A countrywoman with three schoolchildren, Mary Norwak has written about food for the *Daily Express*, *The Times* and *The Guardian*, and is now a contributor to *House and Garden* and *The Lady*. She is also cookery editor of *Farmers' Weekly* and editor of *Freezer World*.

Also by Mary Norwak

Mary Norwak

Crockpot Cooking

Futura Publications Limited
A Futura Book

033488

A Futura Book

First published by Futura Publications
Limited in 1977, reprinted 1978, 1979, 1980

ISBN 0 8600 7579 6
Printed in Great Britain by
Hazell Watson & Viney Ltd
Aylesbury, Bucks

Futura Publications Limited
110 Warner Road
Camberwell, London SE5

Contents

Introduction

When I was first introduced to crockpot cooking, I tended to disbelieve the fact that it could add anything to my life. As a working mother, I have the advantage of doing most of my work at home, but writing needs intense concentration and I tend to 'switch off' for long hours at a stretch. The family comes roaring home in the early evening and if I'm completely absorbed in a job, they end up with a quick grill or something I've just about remembered to put in the oven earlier in the day. Frankly, during a working week, there is little time to plan meals economically or fill the oven to capacity.

Now we have the crockpot as a marvellous extra tool in the kitchen, and I can feel smug when I produce my work *and* a tasty meal at the end of the day. A few minutes around break-fast-time assembling and pre-browning ingredients are re-warded by a nourishing and delicious meal some eight or ten hours later. On other occasions, a simple salad can be preceded by a hearty soup or completed by a satisfying pudding. The great joy of the crockpot is that it never needs watching. With other methods of cooking, food has to be checked from time to time to see that it isn't drying out or browning too much, or even burning or sticking. Food in the crockpot does not need stirring or checking during cooking and there is no need to hang around in the kitchen. Indeed, the temptation to lift the lid and inspect the contents must be firmly resisted or it re-sults in longer cooking times. I can then remain happily slaving over a hot typewriter as long as I like, and don't even need to worry if I work away from home for a day. For those who don't need to work, the crockpot still has enormous advantages, giving time for other work around the house, for gardening or other favourite hobbies, or for being away from home on occa-sions.

Before starting on the recipes in this book, take a little time to read the guides to crockpot cooking, raw materials, prepara-

7

tion and planning. The techniques of using a crockpot success-fully are a little different from those used in conventional cooking, but favourite recipes can be quickly adapted to crock-pot methods when the basic technique has been learned. Classical recipes may not be prepared quite according to classic methods but results can still be very good, and food prepared this way is full of flavour and nourishment. Keep your manu-facturer's instruction book on hand as cooking methods vary slightly in different models.

My particular thanks are due to Tower Housewares Ltd, The Prestige Group Ltd and Kenwood Manufacturing Co. Ltd for their help in preparing this book.

MARY NORWAK

Portions
Recipes will serve 4–6, according to appetite.

Metrication
Recipes in this book are scaled to the 25 g/ounce and 25 ml/ fluid ounce recommended for cooking purposes by the Metri-cation Board to avoid awkward calculations, and these are adjusted in recipes to allow for the difference between the approved scale and the exact conversion. When canned foods are used in a recipe, use the size which is nearest to your recipe, though it may differ slightly in weight. In crockpot recipes, a slight variation in the weight of ingredients will not affect the finished result, whereas the proportions of solid and liquid in baking are of great importance.

Part One

GUIDE TO CROCKPOT COOKING

Crockpot cookery is an up-to-date version of a traditional method of cooking used by our ancestors who knew the value of leaving their stews to cook gently for hours in an earthenware container in a low oven. Their dishes were full of flavour and nourishment and the meat and vegetables were succulent and tender. The crockpot provides the same advantages, giving dishes which will not stick, burn, boil over or overcook, and which can be left for many hours to cook slowly.

The crockpot runs on about the same amount of current which is needed for an electric light bulb. In fact, cooking in a conventional oven does not use a great deal of fuel compared with the use of other appliances in the house such as water heaters, but often there is little time to fill an oven economically with a number of dishes and it certainly always seems wasteful to switch on the oven to cook only one casserole.

TYPES OF CROCKPOTS

There are a number of different crockpots available, differing slightly in construction and cooking methods, but the basic principles are the same. The food is cooked in a container which provides wraparound heat, thus avoiding the overcooking which can result from bottom-heat only. The food is sealed into the crockpot with a well-fitting lid which prevents evaporation, and the food cooks gently in the liquid which results from the steam on the lid and casserole wall condensing. This gives richly-flavoured dishes which retain full food value.

Basically the crockpot consists of a stoneware food container wrapped around by a metal casing containing heating elements controlled by a two-position switch giving HIGH and LOW settings. The lid, feet, handles and switch are heat-resistant. In some models the stoneware pot is detachable from the crockpot for service and may be used under the grill or in the oven to finish dishes – this stoneware container is replaceable in case of damage.

Earthenware is a poor conductor of heat and therefore a good insulator, and heat transfer to the food is slow. The earthenware portion of the crockpot is constructed of a thickness most suitable for slow heat transfer, so an even temperature is maintained during cooking and food remains hot after cooking while waiting to be served.

The size of available crockpots is variable, so it is a good idea to check the capacity with the manufacturer's booklet and see how many recipes in this book compare with their recommended quantities before you prepare a recipe or double a recipe for freezing purposes. Crockpots may be filled to within ½ in./ 12 mm of the rim without risk of spillage.

FOOD HYGIENE

Because a crockpot cools down very slowly, it is most important that food should never be left to cool in the container. Leftover food should be put into a clean container, covered and refrigerated. Raw materials should never be prepared and left in the crockpot ready to start cooking early the next day. Ingredients may of course be cut up and stored in the refrigerator, but should only be put into the crockpot when the heat is switched on.

The cooking temperatures of a crockpot are completely safe and present no health hazards, if certain precautions are observed. See that frozen meat, poultry or fish is completely thawed before putting into the crockpot. Frozen vegetables should be slightly thawed before adding to a dish during cooking so that they do not reduce the cooking temperature drastically. Do not try to reheat frozen foods in a crockpot, and do not use it for reheating already cooked dishes. Follow manufacturer's instructions carefully if pre-heating of the crockpot is recommended, or hot liquids should be added, or food should be cooked on HIGH for a short time before switching to LOW setting for longer slow cooking.

PREPARING THE CROCKPOT

See that the crockpot is wired correctly according to manufacturer's instructions. Before using a crockpot for the first time, make sure it is disconnected from the electricity supply. Rinse the inside of the crockpot and the lid in a little lukewarm soapy water, rinse and dry thoroughly before putting back in position.

Plug the lead into the socket at the base of the crockpot very firmly, and then plug the switch into the electricity socket. Switch on the current and then press the switch to the required setting (some models have an indicator light to show when the crockpot is working).

Once the crockpot is filled and cooking has begun, the lid should not be lifted as this will result in considerable loss of heat and steam. Towards the end of cooking time, the lid may be lifted briefly to introduce quick-cooking vegetables or thickening for gravy.

CROCKPOT CARE AND MAINTENANCE

Keep the crockpot on a level flat surface where it cannot be accidentally moved, touched or tipped over. Do not let the cord get entangled or let it touch the outer surface of the crockpot.

For cleaning, a crockpot must never be submerged in water. A detachable stoneware pot can easily be cleaned in warm soapy water. If the inner pot is a permanent fixture, it can be filled with warm soapy water and left to soak for a while, before careful rinsing and drying. Crockpots must be completely dried and should be stored so that there is free circulation of air to the pot. The outside casing should be wiped with a warm damp cloth and dried, and no abrasive pad or powder should be used. Be careful not to subject the crockpot to sudden changes of temperature by putting in very cold food or cold water when the pot is hot. Don't ever scrape at the crockpot with a sharp implement which might scratch the glaze on the stoneware and provide a breeding ground for bacteria. If a slight 'bloom' occurs on the inside of the stoneware pot in hard water areas, this can be removed with a mild liquid cleaner, or with a soft nylon scouring pad. When the bloom has been removed, wipe over the surface with a little vegetable oil to restore the sparkle.

To remove a stoneware pot from the outer casing, use oven gloves or a cloth to hold it, and be careful not to hit the pot or lid on water taps or sink edges. Avoid putting the stoneware pot or the outer casing over a naked flame, and always put the hot pot on a table mat or wooden board, not on a cold surface.

Part Two
GUIDE TO RAW MATERIALS

While conventional recipes can easily be adapted to crockpot cookery, there are a few points to note about the behaviour of some raw materials during this method of slow-cooking. This can mean that ingredients have to be prepared in a slightly different way or added later in a recipe than with traditional methods.

MEAT

Beef, lamb, pork, veal and offal can all be prepared in the crockpot. If frozen, meat must be completely thawed before cooking. For the best flavour and texture, brown the meat in a little fat in a separate pan before putting into the crockpot, and drain off excess fat. Browning meat helps to cut down the fat content, which will help those on a fat-free diet. This pre-cooking also seals the surfaces of the meat so that juices are not drawn out completely into the cooking liquid, which can result in stringy texture and poor flavour.

POULTRY AND GAME

The same rules apply to poultry and game as to meat. They must always be completely thawed before cooking. The slow-cooking method is particularly good for preparing older poultry or game. Small whole birds may be cooked, or individual portions. When cooking duck, a large quantity of fat will be released and this should be strained off the dish before completion and serving.

FISH

Fish can be spoiled by overcooking, but it is very good if cooked carefully in the crockpot. Delicate flavours develop slowly and subtly and all flavour and nutritive value is sealed inside the crockpot, while fish remains firm-textured and is easy to lift from the pot. Solid fish such as cod or haddock are good for crockpot cookery, and oily fish such as herring and mackerel respond well to the slow method of cooking in many traditional dishes in which the fish is prepared in cider or vinegar. Rolled fish fillets and fish steaks are particularly suitable for crockpot cookery, and large quantities can be fitted into the crockpot. Seafood, such as shrimps or prawns, is normally cooked when bought, and should only be added about 30 minutes before serving time to fish dishes.

CHEESE

Hard cheeses do not respond well to long slow cooking, and for cheese flavour it is better to use processed cheese or cheese spread.

VEGETABLES

Vegetables need particular attention in preparation as they require longer cooking than meat in the crockpot. Root vegetables, including potatoes, should be cut in thin slices or small cubes and are best placed at the bottom of the crockpot under the meat or poultry. Peas and sweetcorn cook more quickly and can be added 45 or 30 minutes before serving time, according to circumstances. Frozen vegetables may be used in crockpot recipes but have already been part-cooked during the blanching process, so may be added in the same way as peas and corn. So that frozen vegetables do not reduce the temperature of the dish too much, they should be partly thawed before putting into the crockpot.

Dried vegetables can give useful flavouring to dishes – onions, peppers and mixed vegetables are particularly handy for casseroles. They may be added with other ingredients, but instructions on the pack should be referred to in case pre-soaking is necessary.

Since there is no evaporation in crockpot cooking, vegetables develop their full flavours and this can be very strong. When adapting conventional recipes to crockpot cookery, cut the amount of strongly flavoured vegetables such as onions, leeks, peppers and turnips by about half. Leaf vegetables such as cabbage and spinach are not suitable for slow cooking as they lose colour and flavour. The exception is red cabbage, traditionally cooked in a casserole.

DRIED PULSES

Dried peas, beans and lentils can present a problem in crockpot cookery. Canned beans, such as kidney or butter beans, may be drained and added to meat dishes for speed and to ensure a tender result. If you prefer to use the dried varieties, preparation is necessary so that the peas or beans will become soft during slow cooking. Pulses may be soaked overnight before adding to the other ingredients, but the results are not generally good. For a smooth soup, pulses may be crushed in a powerful blender before cooking, or whole pulses may be cooked on their own in a crockpot overnight before draining and proceeding with a recipe in which they are incorporated.

A quicker way of getting good results is to put pulses into cold water, bring them to the boil and cook for 2–3 minutes before taking off the heat, covering and leaving to stand for an hour. About 2½ pints/1·5 l of water will be needed to cook 1 lb/450 g beans or peas; then add them to the crockpot recipe.

PASTA AND RICE

Pasta (macaroni, spaghetti, noodles or pasta shapes) should be boiled for about 5 minutes before adding to the crockpot. The pasta should be just softened, not completely cooked. If un-cooked pasta is added to dishes, the starch grains will burst, gelatinize, and absorb liquids, and the pieces of pasta will clump together.

Long-grain rice can be used for all-day cooking, and should be put in with the other ingredients. About ¼ pint/150 ml extra liquid should be added for each 4 oz/100 g rice apart from the liquid already in the recipe. Quick-cooking rice may be used for crockpot recipes. Cooked rice can be added to recipes during cooking, and then no additional liquid will be required.

HERBS AND SPICES

Use fresh herbs and spices whenever possible, as stale dried ones develop an off-flavour during cooking. Whole herbs and spices are always preferable for flavour and can be removed just before serving. When dried ground herbs have to be used, add them during the final hour of cooking. Check seasoning before serving. Be particularly careful with salt in recipes if bacon, ham or stock cubes are used as these can be very salty and this becomes concentrated during crockpot cooking.

MILK AND CREAM

Milk, cream and commercial soured cream can break down during long low cooking, causing separation or curdling, and it is usually best to add these towards the end of cooking time.

FATS

Fats do not 'bake off' in a crockpot as they would in a conventional oven. Make sure surplus fat is trimmed from meat before cooking, and if possible fry the meat lightly and drain off surplus fat before putting the meat into the crockpot. Excess fat in a crockpot can cause an increase in temperature and affect cooking times.

LIQUIDS

Because of the slow cooking in a crockpot, there is little evaporation and consequent loss of liquid. Usually $\frac{1}{4}$–$\frac{1}{2}$ pint/ 150–300 ml liquid will be enough in most meat recipes. Meat will look browner when small amounts of liquids are used, and the flavour of cooking liquids will become very concentrated. Too much liquid can cause a rise in temperature which will affect cooking times. Liquid can be water, stock, cider, beer, wine, or the liquid from canned tomatoes. A stock cube can be used if stock is not available, but seasoning should be adjusted as stock cubes can be very salty. Condensed soups can be used as the cooking liquid in crockpots will give flavour and thickening.

Part Three

PLANNING AND PREPARATION

Methods of preparation in the various available crockpots are slightly different but the basic principles remain the same. The food is prepared ready for service and cooked on low heat so that it can be ready for eating in six or seven hours without further attention. The crockpot is attractive and practical for service at table, and meals for latecomers can safely be kept warm on low heat for an hour or two past the main mealtime. Always check with manufacturer's instructions before experimenting with crockpot cookery, but follow these general principles for complete success.

TEMPERATURE CONTROL

It is recommended that some crockpots should be pre-heated for a maximum of 20 minutes on HIGH setting with the lid on while the ingredients are being prepared. Some manufacturers also recommend that the food should be cooked on HIGH setting for a short time before switching to LOW for long slow cooking (I prefer this method and have indicated it in the recipes in this book). To speed up a meal, recipes may be cooked on HIGH throughout, and will be ready in just over half the time recommended on LOW. This means that meals are adaptable for midday or evening service – a casserole prepared at breakfast-time will be ready in the middle of the day if cooked on HIGH, but may safely be left on LOW setting all day ready for service in the early evening. If timing has to be more delicately adjusted for a meal, it is possible to vary the settings to suit your circumstances. If you want a meal at

8 p.m. for example, but the recipe indicates it will take 10–12 hours on LOW setting, and you cannot start cooking until midday, start the crockpot on HIGH for 2 hours, then continue cooking on LOW for 6 hours.

Factors affecting temperature

Very cold room temperatures or a direct draught will affect the cooking performance of a crockpot, particularly on LOW setting. If these conditions cannot be avoided, use the HIGH setting. Sometimes voltage reductions, particularly in cold weather or at peak cooking times, can affect the electricity supply. This may affect cooking times, and it may be necessary to allow a little extra time for cooking.

It is most important to keep the lid on the crockpot, as every time the lid is removed steam is released which helps to cook the food from the top. It takes 15–20 minutes to regain the lost steam and temperature when the lid has been put back, and obviously this can add considerably to the necessary cooking time.

Large or small quantities

Larger or smaller quantities may be cooked, but cooking times will vary slightly. Food will not overcook in the crockpot. The times shown in the recipes are applicable when the crockpot is at least half-filled. When altering the quantity of recipes, allow a little longer than you think necessary, because halving a recipe, for instance, will not halve the cooking time – root vegetables in particular take a long time to cook. Mixed meat-and-vegetable dishes will take at least 6 hours in the crockpot on LOW setting, even if smaller quantities are cooked than specified in recipes.

FOOD PREPARATION

If your crockpot needs pre-heating according to manufacturer's instructions, switch on the crockpot while preparing ingredients. Assemble all items before starting to cut up or heat ingredients.

Browning meat and vegetables

While it is possible to prepare most crockpot recipes by One-Step Cooking (see below), the quality, texture and flavour of dishes is greatly improved by pre-browning some ingredients. This cannot be done in the crockpot, but requires a frying pan or heavy saucepan. Meat and poultry should be cut in pieces as specified in the recipes and browned in fat until the surfaces are sealed and light golden in colour. This helps to seal in flavour and to give a firm texture. Without pre-browning, flesh becomes ragged and all the flavour seeps out into the cooking liquid. Onions improve in flavour from pre-browning, and other vegetables may also be briefly cooked in the same fat. For some dishes, the fat should be completely drained off the food, but a little flour can be cooked in the fat and the cooking liquid added and boiled before adding to the crockpot. This will save thickening gravy later if time is likely to be short. Pre-browning not only improves the appearance and flavour of the finished dish, but also helps to boost the cooking temperature of the food.

Adding liquid

Some manufacturer's instructions indicate that liquid should be brought to the boil before adding to the crockpot. This again helps to boost the cooking temperature of the food. It will be noticed that the amount of liquid used in crockpot recipes is somewhat less than in conventional recipes. This is because the food cooks in the steam which condenses on the lid and casserole rim and there is no evaporation or heat loss. When adapting your own favourite recipes, cut the liquid by about half – usually $\frac{1}{4}-\frac{1}{2}$ pint/150–300 ml will be enough for the crockpot.

Stirring

It is not necessary to stir food in the crockpot while on the LOW setting. Steam condenses on the lid and casserole rim which forms a water seal which keeps the heat in and cooks the food. If the lid is lifted off, it will take 15–20 minutes to build up the steam and temperature again which will affect cooking time considerably. Hard root vegetables need to remain at the bottom of the crockpot for thorough cooking, but the casserole may be stirred about 30 minutes before serving time to distribute ingredients evenly or to add thickening to gravy. There is no risk of food sticking or burning in the crockpot, but dishes containing rice or pasta cooked on HIGH setting can be stirred once to prevent the rice or pasta clumping together.

Thickening sauce and gravy

If ingredients have been pre-browned, flour may be cooked in the fat which will form a roux to thicken the gravy or sauce. However, with one-step cooking, it may be necessary to add some thickening. Tomato or vegetable purée will help to thicken gravy and may be included at the beginning of cooking. Condensed canned soup used as liquid in a casserole will also add its own thickening, and may be put with the other ingredients at the beginning of the cooking process. Recipes containing potatoes, pasta or rice will also probably yield a thick enough gravy without further attention.

To thicken a gravy at the later stage of cooking, add cornflour or plain flour (about $\frac{1}{2}$ oz/15 g) made into a paste with water. Alternatively work equal quantities of butter and flour together to form a paste and stir this into the liquid in the crockpot. These additions should be made about 45–30 minutes before serving time, and should be stirred in well. .

Finishing a dish

If your crockpot has a detachable stoneware pot inside the casing, your range of recipes is considerably widened. Mashed potatoes or a topping of sliced cooked potatoes, or pastry can be placed on a meat filling and cooked near the top of a hot oven. A potato topping can be quickly browned and crisped under a hot grill. If you want to try cooking a pasta recipe such as lasagne or macaroni cheese in the crockpot, it will be only a pale imitation of the oven-baked dish, but with a detachable stoneware pot the surface can be quickly browned under a grill when cooking is completed.

Dumplings are a useful and economical addition to casseroles and need about 30 minutes cooking on HIGH setting before serving. Even if the crockpot has been on LOW setting for some hours to cook the casserole, it must be switched to HIGH before the dumplings are added.

Garnishes such as chopped parsley, olives, fried or toasted bread cubes, slices of toasted French bread or hot scones can be put on top of the contents of the crockpot just before serving. Cream or commercial soured cream may be stirred into the crockpot just before serving.

Cooling and storing

Leftover food must never be left to cool in the crockpot, nor must it be left in a crockpot for storage in a refrigerator or freezer. As soon as the meal has been finished, remove any leftovers and put them into a clean container. Cover and cool quickly and store in the refrigerator.

Cooking for freezing

With a large crockpot, it is possible to cook a casserole which will yield two family meals. Serve the first meal, then put the other portion into a freezer container, cool quickly and freeze. Do not add cream or commercial soured cream to dishes which are to be frozen – if they are in the recipe, take out the freezer portion before finishing the dish for immediate serving. With a smaller crockpot, the same method can be used to yield two meals for a small family.

ONE-STEP COOKING

Many people will find one-step cooking in the crockpot very useful, although the appearance and flavour may not be quite so good as when food is pre-browned. The general method for one-step cooking is to cut all root vegetables in small pieces and to prepare the meat or poultry. Put the vegetables in the bottom of the crockpot, add the other ingredients and pour in boiling liquid. Cover with the lid and cook on LOW, but add 2–3 hours to the time given for recipes in which ingredients have been pre-browned. Thickening may be added 30 minutes before serving time.

MENU PLANNING

Crockpot cooking is ideal for both family meals and for entertaining, and a delicious and nutritious menu can easily be assembled based on the crockpot recipe as the main item. It is pointless to use the crockpot to save time and fuel and then to light the oven to produce accompanying dishes, so a menu should be planned to accommodate quick-cooking accompaniments or pre-cooked items.

Soup

If the crockpot has been used for a soup, this will probably be a hearty one which is almost a meal in itself. There need only be an accompaniment of fresh crusty bread or rolls. Cheese can be added if liked, with fresh fruit to follow. For a bigger meal, the soup can be followed by a salad with cold meat, poultry, egg or cheese, or with grilled meat or fish accompanied by a salad.

Main Course

If the crockpot has been used for a main course, it may already contain plenty of vegetables. It takes only about 15 minutes to boil water and cook rice, pasta or potatoes. Additional vegetables will take about the same time, or a salad can be served. The second course may be fresh fruit and cheese, an ice or a cold pudding, or a quickly-cooked dish such as pancakes or poached fruit. For a meal suitable for guests, a fruit or seafood cocktail makes a good first course, or meat or fish pâté prepared 24 hours beforehand.

Sweet Course

If the crockpot has been used for a sweet course, this may fit into a menu in two ways. A dish such as poached fruit or fruit in wine can be prepared on one day and chilled for use the next day to follow a savoury crockpot dish. If a hot pudding occupies the crockpot all day, it can make a filling finish to a salad meal, or to a bread and cheese course, or to toasted sandwiches or other quickly-cooked snacks.

Timing a Menu

However you wish to use the crockpot to aid meal-planning, be sure to plan the timing of meals carefully. Try to organize your shopping, thaw any frozen food, and allow enough time for the complete cooking of the dish. If you are entertaining guests, prepare first and third courses the evening before and store them in the refrigerator, or remove frozen dishes from the freezer first thing in the morning to thaw slowly in the refrigerator during the day.

If you know that the family will be wanting a quick meal in the evening, or guests will arrive soon after your return home, prepare the table in the morning. That will leave you free for the necessary 15–20 minutes to cook accompanying vegetables, make a salad, heat bread or add garnishes to the crockpot dish.

Part Four
RECIPES

Soups

The crockpot is ideal for making soup which benefits from long slow cooking. Home-made soup is very economical and can provide a nourishing but cheap complete meal with crusty or wholemeal bread. Some cheese and fresh fruit can be added for those who are still hungry. In most soups, the ingredients may be simply placed in the stockpot and left to cook slowly for many hours, but the flavour is improved if vegetables are lightly cooked in butter or oil before the liquid is added, and this must be done in a separate saucepan before the partly-cooked vegetables are put into the crockpot. The liquid may be water or stock, and the crockpot can be used for making over-night stock from fresh bones, cooked carcass bones or vegetables. DO NOT USE THE CROCKPOT AS A PERMANENT STOCKPOT; stock should be freshly made, cooled quickly and stored in the refrigerator for use.

Vegetables take surprisingly long to cook in a crockpot and it is a good idea to place root vegetables in the base of the crockpot, topping them with onions, cabbage, beans and so on. It is best to cut vegetables in thin slices or small dice. If you are adapting your own favourite recipes, you may want to cut down a little on the very strongly flavoured vegetables such as onions or turnips, as their flavour can become very concentrated in the crockpot. If you like a smooth soup, rub the cooked contents of the crockpot through a sieve, or blend them in a liquidizer, and return the smooth soup to a washed crockpot for reheating before service.

Rice and barley may be cooked in soup in the crockpot, but pasta is best slightly cooked (about 5 minutes) before adding to the other ingredients. Dried beans, dried peas and lentils are not totally satisfactory if soaked overnight in the conventional manner. I find it best to cook them for a short time, then cover and leave to stand for an hour before using with their cooking liquid in a recipe (exact times are given in individual recipes). Season soups carefully, and check seasoning before service. This is particularly important when using bacon or ham in a soup recipe, as these may be over-salted, and additional salt should be used with care.

MAKING BASIC STOCK

Many soups and other savoury dishes benefit from the use of stock rather than water. Stock cubes may be used with water, but often these are heavily seasoned, particularly with salt, and all dishes cooked with them tend to taste the same. Basic stocks may be made in the crockpot and the long slow cooking will draw out the flavour of the ingredients, making richly-flavoured stock. The steam produced by this method adds to the liquid, so ingredients should only just be covered with water before cooking. For very concentrated stock, put in less water and put a piece of foil on top of the ingredients. When making stock, cook on LOW for 12–16 hours. Strain and cool the stock quickly and take off any fat when cold. Store in the refrigerator if not being used immediately.

Meat Stock

2–3 lb/1–1.5 kg bones
1 medium onion
½ small turnip
2 medium carrots
1 celery stick
Salt
Sprig of parsley
Sprig of thyme
1 bayleaf

Fresh beef or veal bones are best to use, but bones from a cooked dish such as a joint may be used. For dark brown stock, brown the bones and onion in hot fat in a thick pan before putting into the crockpot. To make the stock, put the bones and finely chopped vegetables into the crockpot with the herbs and water to cover. Cover and cook on LOW for 12–16 hours. Strain and cool the stock quickly and store in the refrigerator.

Poultry Stock

Use the poultry carcass, skin and trimmings and giblets instead of meat bones.

Fish Stock

Fish bones, trimmings and skin
Sprig of parsley
Sprig of thyme
1 bayleaf
Salt
1 small onion
1 piece of lemon rind

Put all the ingredients into the crockpot and cover with water. Cover and cook on LOW for 12 hours. Strain and cool quickly and store in the refrigerator. Use within 24 hours.

Vegetable Stock

1 lb/500 g onions
1 lb/500 g carrots
3 celery sticks
Salt and pepper
Sprig of parsley
Sprig of thyme
1 bayleaf
3 pints/1.5 l water

Peel the onions and chop them roughly. Peel and chop the carrots, and chop the celery. Put all the ingredients into the crockpot, cover and cook on LOW for 8 hours. Strain, cool and store in the refrigerator.

Cauliflower soup

1 medium cauliflower
1 medium onion
1 celery stick
Salt and pepper
2 pints/1 l chicken stock
¼ pint/125 ml single cream
1 teaspoon/5 ml Worcestershire sauce

Trim the cauliflower and cut into flowerets. Peel the onion and
chop finely. Chop the celery finely. Put the cauliflower, onion,
celery, seasoning and stock into the crockpot, cover and cook
on LOW for 6–7 hours. Sieve the soup or liquidize in a blender.
Return to the crockpot and stir in the cream and Worcestershire sauce. Heat on HIGH for 10 minutes.

Celery soup

6 celery sticks
1 oz/25 g butter
1 oz/25 g plain flour
½ pint/300 ml water
½ pint/300 ml milk
Salt and pepper
Pinch of nutmeg
1 bayleaf

Chop the celery sticks very finely and cook in the butter for 5 minutes. Stir in the flour and then the water and milk. Bring to the boil, stirring well. Put into the crockpot with salt and pepper, a pinch of nutmeg and the bayleaf. Cook on LOW for 4 hours. Remove the bayleaf before serving.

Leek and potato soup

1 oz/25 g butter
8 oz/225 g potatoes
2 lb/1 kg leeks
1 pint/500 ml chicken stock
Salt and pepper
¼ pint/150 ml milk
1 tablespoon/15 ml chopped chives

Peel the potatoes and cut them in thin slices. Clean the leeks, trim the tops, and cut into thin slices. Melt the butter and cook the vegetables for 3 minutes. Stir in the stock, season well, and bring to the boil. Put into the crockpot, cover and cook on HIGH for 15 minutes, then continue cooking on LOW for 6 hours. Stir in the milk and cook on HIGH for 30 minutes. Serve sprinkled with chopped chives. If liked, the soup may be liquidized in a blender before reheating with the milk.

Onion soup

12 oz/350 g onions
2 oz/50 g butter
2 tablespoons/30 ml oil
1 teaspoon/5 ml salt
1 teaspoon/5 ml sugar
1 oz/25 g plain flour
1 pint/500 ml beef stock
Salt and pepper
4 rounds French bread
4 oz/100 g grated Cheddar cheese

Peel the onions and slice them thinly. Melt the butter and oil and fry the onions for 3 minutes. Add the salt and sugar and cook until the onions are golden and soft, but without browning. Put the onions into the crockpot. Stir the flour into the remaining fat and stir in the stock until the mixture is smooth and hot. Pour over the onions and season with salt and pepper. Cover and cook on LOW for 6–7 hours. Just before serving, toast the bread and top with grated cheese. Grill until the cheese has just melted. Put a piece of the toast in the bottom of each bowl before serving the soup. A little Worcestershire sauce, or sherry, may be added to the soup just before serving.

Watercress soup

2 bunches watercress
8 oz/225 g potatoes
1 leek
2 oz/50 g butter
2 pints/1 l chicken stock
Salt and pepper
¼ pint/150 ml milk
2 tablespoons/30 ml single cream

Trim any pieces of root from the watercress and remove any discoloured leaves. Reserve a few large watercress leaves, and chop the rest of the bunches. Put into the crockpot with finely chopped potatoes. Chop the leek finely and cook in the butter until golden. Add to the crockpot with the chicken stock, salt and pepper. Cover and cook on LOW for 6–7 hours. Blend in a liquidizer until smooth. Return to the crockpot with the milk and reheat on LOW for 45 minutes. Stir in the cream and the reserved watercress leaves just before serving.

Sweetcorn soup

1 lb/500 g canned sweetcorn kernels
2 medium potatoes
1 medium onion
Salt and pepper
1 pint/500 ml chicken stock
½ pint/300 ml milk
2 oz/50 g butter
Pinch of nutmeg

Drain the sweetcorn. Put the kernels into the crockpot with finely chopped potatoes and onion, salt and pepper and chicken stock. Cover and cook on LOW for 7–8 hours, Blend the mixture in a liquidizer to a smooth purée. Return to the crockpot with the milk, butter and nutmeg and cover and cook on LOW for 45 minutes. A little chopped parsley may be sprinkled on each portion when serving.

Tomato soup

1½ lb/700 g tomatoes
1 oz/25 g butter
1 small onion
2 medium carrots
2 celery sticks
2 oz/50 g bacon
Sprig of parsley
Sprig of thyme
1 bayleaf
1 pint/500 ml water
1 teaspoon/5 ml sugar
Salt and pepper
¼ pint/150 ml milk
2 tablespoons/30 ml single cream
1 tablespoon/15 ml chopped parsley

Dip the tomatoes into boiling water and remove their skins. Cut the tomatoes in quarters and put into the crockpot. Chop the onion finely. Cut the carrots in thin slices, and chop the celery finely. Melt the butter and fry the vegetables together with the chopped bacon until they are soft and golden. Put into the crockpot with the herbs. Add boiling water, sugar, salt and pepper. Cover and cook on LOW for 8–9 hours. Sieve the soup and return to the crockpot with the milk. Reheat on LOW and stir in the cream just before serving and sprinkle with freshly chopped parsley.

Summer vegetable soup

6 spring onions
2 medium carrots
1 small cauliflower
8 oz/225 g French beans
1 medium potato
1 teaspoon/5 ml chopped parsley
Pinch of thyme
Salt and pepper
3 pints/1½ l chicken stock

Cut the onions in very thin slices. Slice the carrots finely and cut the beans into 1 in/2.5 cm pieces. Break the cauliflower into small pieces and dice the potato. Put all the vegetables into the crockpot with the herbs, seasoning and chicken stock. Cover and cook on LOW for 7–8 hours. Serve with fried or toasted bread cubes or a sprinkling of crumbled crisply cooked bacon.

Vegetable soup

2 large onions
5 celery sticks
5 medium carrots
1 lb/450 g tomatoes
3 pints/1·5 l beef stock
Salt and pepper

Peel the onions and chop them finely. Chop the celery and cut the carrots in very thin slices. Dip the tomatoes in boiling water and remove the skins. Cut in pieces and take out the pips. Mix the vegetables together in the crockpot. Bring the stock to the boil and pour into the crockpot. Season with salt and pepper, cover and cook on LOW for 8 hours. Serve with fried or toasted bread cubes.

Winter vegetable soup

1 oz/25 g butter
2 lb/1 kg root vegetables
1 oz/25 g plain flour
1½ pints/750 ml beef stock
Salt and pepper
Pinch of mixed herbs

Use a mixture of carrots, onions, potatoes, parsnips, turnips and celery, according to what is available. Peel the vegetables and chop them very finely. Melt the butter and cook the vegetables gently for 3 minutes. Stir in the flour and add the stock. Bring to the boil. Season to taste and add the herbs. Put into the crockpot, cover and cook on HIGH for 30 minutes. Continue cooking on LOW for 6 hours.

Minestrone

2 oz/50 g streaky bacon
1 small onion
1 leek
1 oz/25 g butter
1 garlic clove
1 tablespoon/15 ml chopped parsley
½ small cabbage
1 potato
4 oz/100 g French beans
2 celery sticks
2 small carrots
1 oz/25 g long grain rice
1¼ pints/650 ml stock

Chop the bacon and heat in a thick pan until the fat begins to run. Slice the onion thickly and chop the leek and add to the bacon with the butter. Cook gently until the vegetables are golden. Put into the crockpot with the crushed garlic, parsley, finely-shredded cabbage and diced potatoes. Slice the beans (frozen ones may be used but should be thawed before adding to the crockpot), dice the celery and slice the carrots thinly. Add to the crockpot with the rice, seasoning and stock. Stir well, cover and cook on LOW for 10–11 hours. If liked, pasta may be used instead of rice, but cook spaghetti shapes or macaroni for 5 minutes before draining and adding to the crockpot with the other ingredients.

Creole soup

1 medium onion
1 small green pepper
2 oz/50 g butter
1½ oz/40 g plain flour
2 pints/1 l beef stock
1 lb/500 g tomatoes
Salt andpepper
Pinch of sugar
2 oz/50 g spaghetti rings
1 teaspoon/5 ml vinegar
1 teaspoon/5 ml horseradish sauce

Chop the onion and pepper very finely and soften in the butter. When the onion is golden, stir in the flour and cook for 2 minutes. Stir in the stock and bring to the boil, stirring all the time, then put into the crockpot. Dip the tomatoes into boiling water and remove their skins. Cut the tomatoes in half and remove the seeds, then cut the flesh in small pieces. Put the tomatoes into the crockpot with the salt, pepper and sugar. Cook the spaghetti rings in boiling water for 3 minutes, drain and add to the crockpot together with the vinegar and horseradish sauce. Cover and cook on LOW for 6–7 hours.

Kidney soup

8 oz/225 g ox kidney
1 oz/25 g butter
1 small onion
1 oz plain flour
1 small carrot
2 pints/1 l beef stock
Sprig of parsley
Sprig of thyme
1 bayleaf
Salt and pepper
1 tablespoon/15 ml sherry

Cut the kidney in thin slices. Melt the butter and cook the kidney and finely sliced onion until the onion is soft and golden. Stir in the flour and continue cooking for 2 minutes. Add the finely chopped carrot and stock, and bring to the boil, stirring well. Put into the crockpot with the herbs and seasoning. Cover and cook on LOW for 8–9 hours. Blend in a liquidizer until smooth. Return to the crockpot, stir in the sherry, and reheat on LOW for 30 minutes.

Oxtail soup

1 oxtail
½ oz/15 g seasoned flour
2 oz/50 g butter
2 pints/1 l water
2 medium carrots
2 medium onions
1 turnip
1 celery stick
Salt and pepper
½ teaspoon/2·5 ml Worcestershire sauce
½ teaspoon/2·5 ml lemon juice

Cut the oxtail in pieces. Roll in the seasoned flour and fry in the butter until the surfaces are sealed. Put into the crockpot with boiling water and with the vegetables cut in very small pieces. Add the seasoning, cover and cook on LOW for 10–11 hours. Remove the meat from the oxtail bones. Blend the vegetables, meat and liquid in a liquidizer and return to the crockpot. Stir in the Worcestershire sauce and lemon juice, and continue cooking on LOW for 1 hour.

Scotch broth

1 lb/500 g lean neck of lamb
1 leek
2 celery sticks
1 medium onion
1 medium carrot
1 medium turnip
2 oz/50 g pearl barley
Sprig of parsley
Salt and pepper
3 pints/1.5 l water

Cut the meat into small cubes. Slice the leek and celery thinly, and chop the onion, carrot and turnip finely. Put the meat and vegetables into the crockpot with the barley, parsley, seasoning and boiling water. Cover and cook on LOW for 8–9 hours. Remove the sprig of parsley before serving.

Seafood soup

1½ lb/700 g cod or haddock fillets
4 streaky bacon rashers
1 medium onion
2 medium potatoes
Salt and pepper
½ pint/300 ml water
¼ pint/150 ml milk
2 oz/50 g prawns

Cut the fish into 1 in/2·5 cm squares. Frozen fish may be used but should be thawed before use. Chop the bacon and onion. Put the bacon into a pan and heat gently until the fat runs out. Add the onion and cook until golden and soft. Put the onion and bacon into the crockpot. Peel the potatoes, slice them thinly and add to the crockpot. Put in the fish pieces, salt and pepper and hot water. Cover and cook on LOW for 6–7 hours. Thirty minutes before serving, stir in the milk and prawns and continue heating. If this soup is served with plenty of crusty bread, it can make a complete meal.

Summer shrimp soup

1 medium onion
1 oz/25 g butter
1 tablespoon/15 ml curry powder
1 lb/500 g canned tomatoes
2 pints/1 l chicken stock
Pinch of salt
Pinch of celery salt
8 oz/225 g peeled shrimps
2 oz/50 g shelled peas
2 tablespoons/30 ml single cream

Chop the onion very finely and cook gently in the butter until soft. Stir in the curry powder and cook for 1 minute. Put into the crockpot with the tomatoes and their liquid, chicken stock, salt and celery salt. Cover and cook on LOW for 5–6 hours. Sieve the soup to get rid of the tomato pips. Return to the crockpot and add the shrimps and peas. Cover and continue cooking on LOW for 30 minutes. Stir in the cream just before serving.

Country Bean Soup

6 oz/150 g haricot beans
1½ pints/750 ml water
1 large onion
2 medium carrots
1 celery stick
2 tablespoons/30 ml oil
2 garlic cloves
1 bayleaf
1 bacon or ham bone
Salt and pepper
1 tablespoon/15 ml chopped parsley

Put the beans into a saucepan with half the water and bring to
the boil. Simmer for 10 minutes, remove from the heat, cover
and leave to stand for 1 hour. Chop the onion, carrots and
celery finely and cook in the oil until just soft. Put into the
crockpot with the beans and liquid, and add the remaining
water. Put in the crushed garlic, bayleaf and bone, and season
with salt and pepper. If you think the bone may be rather
salty, do not add salt until the soup is cooked when you can
season again to suit your taste. Cover and cook on LOW for
7–8 hours. Remove the bayleaf and bone, and stir in parsley
just before serving.

Ham and Pea Soup

4 oz/100 g split peas
2 pints/1 l water
4 streaky bacon rashers
1 ham or bacon bone
1 leek
1 celery stick
1 bayleaf
Salt and pepper
Pinch of nutmeg

Put the peas into a saucepan with half the water and bring to the boil. Simmer for 2 minutes, remove from the heat, cover and leave to stand for 1 hour. Remove the bacon rind and cut the rashers into small pieces. Cook the bacon in a pan until the fat runs out, and drain off the fat. Put the peas and liquid into the crockpot with the bacon, ham bone, finely sliced leek and celery, bayleaf, salt and pepper, nutmeg and remaining water. Cover and cook on LOW for 8 hours. Take out the ham bone and the bayleaf. Either mash the vegetables into the soup, or liquidize in a blender. Reheat on HIGH for 10–15 minutes. Serve with fried or toasted bread cubes. Be careful with the salt when preparing this recipe, as the ham bone may be rather salty, and it is better to underseason at first and season again just before serving.

Italian Soup

8 oz/225 g red kidney beans
1 pint/500 ml water
2 streaky bacon rashers
1 medium onion
2 celery sticks
1½ pints/750 ml beef stock
2 tomatoes
Pinch of marjoram
1 bayleaf
Salt and pepper
4 oz/100 g short macaroni

Put the beans into a saucepan with the water and bring to the boil. Simmer for 10 minutes, remove from the heat, cover and leave to stand for 1 hour. Chop the bacon and heat until the fat runs. Chop the onion and celery finely and cook with the bacon until the vegetables are soft and golden. Put into the crockpot with the beans and liquid, and beef stock. Peel the tomatoes, remove the pips and cut the flesh into small pieces. Add to the crockpot with the herbs and seasoning. Cook the macaroni in boiling water for 5 minutes, drain and add to the crockpot. Cover and cook on LOW for 8–9 hours. Remove the bayleaf before serving. If liked, a little grated Parmesan cheese may be sprinkled on each serving.

Lentil Soup

1 lb/450 g lentils
2 medium onions
2 medium carrots
2 medium potatoes
6 streaky bacon rashers
4 pints/2 l water
Salt and pepper

Put the lentils into 2 pints/1 l water in a saucepan and bring to the boil. Simmer for 2 minutes, then remove from the heat, cover and leave to stand for 1 hour. Peel the onions and chop them finely. Peel the carrots and potatoes and cut them in very thin slices. Remove the bacon rinds and cut the rashers into small pieces. Put the onions, carrots, potatoes and bacon into the crockpot. Pour over the water and stir in the drained lentils. Season well with salt and pepper. Cover and cook on LOW for 6 hours. Put through a sieve or liquidize in a blender. Taste and add more seasoning if necessary. Reheat and serve sprinkled with some chopped parsley.

Yellow Pea Soup

8 oz/225 g yellow split peas
1 pint/500 ml water
2 celery sticks
1 large carrot
1 medium onion
2 oz/50 g butter
1 tablespoon/15 ml curry powder
1 tablespoon/15 ml lemon juice
1 bayleaf
½ teaspoon/2.5 ml salt
2 pints/1 l chicken stock

Put the split peas into a saucepan with the water and bring to
the boil. Simmer for 2 minutes, remove from the heat, cover
and leave to stand for 1 hour. Chop the celery, carrot and onion
very finely, and soften in the butter. Stir in the curry powder
and cook for 1 minute. Put the vegetable mixture into the
crockpot with the peas and liquid, lemon juice, bayleaf, salt
and chicken stock. Cover and cook on LOW for 8–9 hours. A
little crisply cooked crumbled bacon, or some rings of frank-
furter sausage may be used to garnish this soup.

Pâtés

Home-made pâté is delicious and often far more economical than the bought variety, and it is very useful to serve with salads, or with toast or crusty bread, or as a sandwich filling. To ensure a moist texture, the container of pâté is normally cooked in a baking tin of hot water in a low oven, and the same principle can be applied in a crockpot. A pâté may be made in an earthenware or oven-glass container, a soufflé dish or a metal loaf or cake tin, so be sure to choose one which fits the crockpot easily and allows for hot water to be poured around. The container should be covered with a piece of foil during cooking. To ensure a firm pâté which cuts easily, the top should be covered with a plate or a slightly smaller container after cooking, on which weights should be placed (these can be weights from old-fashioned scales, or cans of food). Pâté is best left under a weight for 24 hours which will give a firm texture and well-blended flavour.

Bacon Pâté

1 large onion
1 lb/450 g boiled bacon
3 oz/75 g fresh white breadcrumbs
1 large egg
¼ pint/150 ml bacon stock
1 tablespoon/15 ml fresh chopped parsley
Pinch of fresh thyme
Pepper

Peel and chop the onion and put through the mincer (fine screen) with the bacon. Mix with the breadcrumbs, beaten egg, stock, herbs and pepper. Put into a greased soufflé dish or loaf tin and cover with a foil lid. Put into the crockpot and pour in boiling water to come half way up the sides of the dish or tin. Cook on HIGH for 4 hours. Remove from the crockpot and cool under a light weight. Serve with toast, or with salad.

Smooth Liver Pâté

1 oz/25 g butter
6 oz/175 g chicken livers
4 oz/100 g pig's liver
1 garlic clove
1 egg
3 tablespoons/45 ml single cream
Salt and pepper
3 bay leaves

Melt the butter. Cut the chicken livers and pig's liver into small pieces and cook in the butter until lightly coloured. Put into a liquidizer with the cooking juices, chopped garlic clove and egg. Blend until smooth. Mix in the cream and seasoning and put into a greased 1 pint/500 ml soufflé dish. Arrange the bay leaves on top and cover the dish with a foil lid. Put the dish into the crockpot and pour in boiling water to come half way up the dish. Cook on HIGH for 30 minutes and then on LOW for 3 hours. Chill before serving with toast.

Country Pâté

6 streaky bacon rashers
6 oz/175 g pork
6 oz/175 g pig's liver
1 small onion
2 oz/50 g white breadcrumbs
1 teaspoon mixed herbs
1 egg
Salt and pepper
Pinch of nutmeg

Remove the rind from the bacon rashers and press out the rashers very thinly with a flat-bladed knife. Line a 1 lb/ 450 g loaf tin with the bacon rashers. Chop the pork, liver and onion very finely and put into a saucepan with just enough water to cover. Simmer for 15 minutes and drain off the cooking liquid if necessary. Season with salt, pepper and nutmeg. This gives a chunky pâté, but the pork and liver may be blended in a liquidizer before mixing with the other ingredients if a smoother pâté is preferred. Put the mixture into the bacon-lined loaf tin, and cover with a piece of foil. Put the loaf tin into the crockpot, and pour boiling water into the crockpot to come half way up the loaf tin. Cook on HIGH for 4 hours. Remove the loaf tin from the crockpot and put a light weight on the surface. Leave in a cold place for the pâté to chill and become firm. Turn out and cut in slices to serve.

Pork and Spinach Terrine

12 oz/350 g cooked spinach
12 oz/350 g lean pork
1 egg
2 tablespoons/30 ml brandy
2 tablespoons/30 ml fresh chopped parsley
1 small onion
Pinch of salt
Pinch of fresh thyme
Pinch of fresh basil
Pinch of ground nutmeg
Pinch of pepper
2 oz/50 g stuffed olives
4 streaky bacon rashers
2 oz/50 g sliced cooked ham
1 bayleaf

Fresh or frozen spinach may be used. Put into a fine-meshed sieve and press out all the liquid until the spinach is very dry. Mince the pork (coarse screen) and mix with the egg, brandy and parsley. Mince the onion (fine screen) and add to the pork. Mix together the salt, thyme, basil, nutmeg and pepper and add half the mixture to the pork. Add the other half of the seasonings to the spinach, together with the chopped olives. Cut the rinds from the bacon rashers, and press the rashers out thinly with a flat-bladed knife. Use these rashers to line a 1 lb/450 g loaf tin. Put in one-third of the pork mixture. Top with half the spinach and then half the ham slices. Top with one-third of the pork mixture, the remaining spinach and ham, and then the remaining pork. Put the bayleaf on top. Cover with a foil lid and place in the crockpot. Put in boiling water to come half way up the tin. Cook on HIGH for 4 hours. Chill under a light weight and cut in slices to serve with salad.

Fish

If fish is overcooked, it loses its juicy tenderness, so that it must be cooked carefully in a crockpot. Overlong cooking shrinks the delicate fibres and makes the flesh tough, so that the fish should be cooked in the crockpot for a shorter time than other foods and should not be left to keep warm longer than the cooking period. When the fish is ready, it should flake easily and still be moist.

Frozen fish may be used for the crockpot, but should be thawed before use. Cooked seafood, such as prawns, is best added towards the end of cooking. It is very convenient to prepare a sauce in the crockpot, adding the seafood while rice is being cooked separately to make a complete meal – this kind of dish is very useful to serve at a buffet meal when the fish in sauce can keep warm while it is being served.

Small whole fish can be cooked in the crockpot and should be laid head-to-tail to fill the space at the bottom of the pot. Fish may be cut in serving portions, or cut in cubes for a casserole, or steaks may be used. Fish may also be rolled around fillings, and rolled fish fillets in a 'souse' of vinegar, ale or cider, are particularly suitable for the slow-cooking method. If carefully timed, fish retains a firm texture and full flavour when prepared in the crockpot.

Herrings in Mustard Cream

4 herrings
2 oz/50 g butter
Salt and pepper
4 teaspoons/20 ml made mustard
3 tablespoons/45 ml tomato purée
¼ pint/150 ml single cream
1 tablespoon/15 ml chopped parsley

Clean the herrings and fillet them, and cut each herring into
two pieces lengthwise. Soften the butter slightly and spread a
little on each piece, and season with salt and pepper. Roll up
each fillet with the skin outside, and place in the crockpot.
Mix the mustard, tomato purée and single cream and pour
over the fish. Cover and cook on HIGH for 2 hours. Sprinkle
with chopped parsley before serving.

Trout in Wine Sauce

4 trout
4 oz/100 g button mushrooms
¼ pint/150 ml dry white wine
1 lemon
Salt and pepper
¼ pint/150 ml double cream

Clean the trout and put them into the crockpot. Chop the mushrooms finely, and put round the fish. Add the wine, the grated rind and juice of the lemon, salt and pepper. Cover and cook on HIGH for 2–3 hours. Stir in the cream and continue cooking for 15 minutes.

Cod in Wine Sauce

½ oz/15 g butter
8 oz/225 g mushrooms
4 cod or haddock steaks
Salt and pepper
4 tablespoons/60 ml dry white wine
2 tablespoons/30 ml lemon juice
1 bayleaf

Grease the crockpot with the butter and put in the mushrooms cut in thin slices. Put in the fish steaks and sprinkle with salt and pepper. Pour on the wine and lemon juice and add the bayleaf. Cover and cook on LOW for 2–3 hours. Take out the bayleaf before serving. Serve with mashed potatoes.

Curried Cod

1½ lb/750 g cod fillets
2 medium onions
1 garlic clove
2 tomatoes
1 oz/25 g chopped parsley
1 tablespoon/15 ml lemon juice
½ oz/15 g curry powder
¼ pint/150 ml dry white wine
Salt and pepper

Cut the cod into 2 in/5 cm squares. Cut the onions in thin slices and crush the garlic. Put the onions and garlic into the crockpot and cover with the pieces of fish. Peel the tomatoes and remove the pips. Cut the flesh into pieces and put on top of the fish. Add the parsley, lemon juice mixed with curry powder, wine and seasoning. Cover and cook on LOW for 2–3 hours. Serve with rice and chutney.

Baked Mackerel

4 mackerel
2 oz/50 g fresh white breadcrumbs
1 lemon
1 teaspoon/5 ml chopped parsley
Pinch of mixed herbs
2 tablespoons/30 ml milk
1 oz/25 g butter
Salt and pepper

Clean the fish and remove the heads and tails. Rub the bread-crumbs very fine. Mix them with the grated lemon rind, parsley and mixed herbs, and bind with the milk. Stuff the cavities of the fish and secure the openings with cocktail sticks. Grease the crockpot and put in the fish, alternating heads and tails. Season with salt and pepper and pour over the juice of the lemon. Cover and cook on LOW for 4–5 hours. Serve with lemon wedges and thin brown bread and butter.

Stuffed Plaice

1½ oz/40 g butter
4 oz/100 g mushrooms
2 hard-boiled eggs
Salt and pepper
8 plaice fillets
1 orange

Heat half the butter and cook the chopped mushrooms for 2 minutes. Chop the eggs and add to the mushrooms with the salt and pepper. Remove the skin from the fillets. Put some mushrooms and egg seasoning on each fillet and roll up firmly. Put into the crockpot and add small pieces of the remaining butter. Add the grated rind and juice of the orange. Cover and cook on LOW for 2–3 hours. A few peeled shrimps or prawns may be added to the stuffing. Serve with new potatoes and peas.

Poached Salmon

2 lb/1 kg salmon
¼ pint/150 ml dry white wine
¼ pint/150 ml water
1 bayleaf
Sprig of parsley
Pinch of salt
1 tablespoon/15 ml lemon juice
½ lemon

Wipe the piece of salmon and put into the crockpot. Pour in the wine and water. Add the bayleaf, parsley, salt, lemon juice and the lemon cut in thin slices. Cover and cook on LOW for 3–4 hours. Serve the salmon with melted butter or Hollandaise sauce.

Soused Herrings

4 herrings
Salt and pepper
1 small onion
8 peppercorns
Sprig of parsley
1 bayleaf
¼ pint/150 ml vinegar
¼ pint/150 ml water

Clean the herrings, removing heads, tails and fins. Take out
the backbones. Season the herrings and roll up from tail end.
Put in the crockpot. Cut the onion into fine rings. Put into a
saucepan with peppercorns, parsley, bayleaf, vinegar and water
and bring to the boil. Pour over the fish and cook on LOW for
4–5 hours. Eat hot, or leave in the cooking liquid until cold,
then chill and serve. Mackerel may be prepared in the same
way, and for mackerel the liquid can be a mixture of cold tea
and white vinegar. The liquid may also be cider, or pale ale for
herring, mackerel or pilchards.

Pacific Fish Casserole

2 tablespoons/30 ml oil
1 small onion
8 oz/225 g canned tomatoes
3 tablespoons/45 ml tomato purée
½ pint/250 ml dry white wine
Pinch of thyme
Pinch of marjoram
Salt and pepper
1 lb/450 g cod, haddock or halibut
8 oz/225 g peeled shrimps
12 mussels or 6 scallops

Heat the oil and cook the finely chopped onion until soft and golden. Stir in the tomatoes and liquid from can, tomato purée, wine, herbs and seasoning, and bring just to the boil. Put into the crockpot with the fish cut into 2 in/5 cm cubes. Cover and cook on LOW for 2–3 hours. Add the shrimps and mussels or scallops and cook on HIGH for 30 minutes. The mussels may be frozen or canned, or they can be fresh, when they can be added in their shells. The scallops should be removed from their shells, the roe detached and added to the casserole together with the white flesh cut into two rounds (frozen scallops may be used but should be thawed first). Serve this casserole with crusty bread, or on a bed of rice.

Summer Fish Casserole

$1\frac{1}{2}$ lb/750 g cod or haddock fillet
1 small onion
8 oz/225 g courgettes
1 bayleaf
Sprig of thyme
Sprig of parsley
Salt and pepper
1 lb/450 g canned tomatoes

Wash and dry the fish and cut it into four or six portions. Chop the onion finely and slice the courgettes thinly without peeling. Put the vegetables into the crockpot and put the pieces of fish on top. Put on the herbs and season well. Chop the tomatoes roughly and pour into the crockpot with the liquid from the can. Cover and cook on LOW for 6–7 hours.

Fish Pudding

1 lb/450 g cod or haddock
3 oz/75 g shredded suet
3 oz/75 g fresh white breadcrumbs
1 tablespoon/15 ml chopped parsley
1 slice onion
2 eggs
½ pint/300 ml milk
Salt and pepper

Remove the skin and bone from the fish and cut the flesh into very small pieces. Mix with the suet, breadcrumbs, chopped parsley and finely chopped onion, beat eggs, milk and seasoning. Put into a greased pudding basin and cover with foil. Put into the crockpot and pour in boiling water to come halfway up the basin. Cover and cook on HIGH for 3–4 hours. Turn out and serve with parsley, tomato or mushroom sauce.

Jambalaya

1 medium onion
1 green pepper
1 celery stick
1 garlic clove
8 oz/225 g slice of gammon
1 lb/450 g canned tomatoes
Pinch of basil
¼ pint/150 ml chicken stock
Salt and pepper
1 lb/450 g shelled prawns
1 lb/450 g cooked rice

Chop the onion, pepper and celery finely and crush the garlic.
Put into the crockpot. Add the ham cut into small cubes. Chop
the tomatoes and add to the crockpot with the liquid from the
can, and the ham. Stir in the basil, chicken stock, salt and
pepper. Cover and cook on LOW for 4–5 hours. Stir in the
prawns and rice and cook on HIGH for 45 minutes. This is a
very good buffet dish served from the crockpot, and accompanied by crusty bread and a green salad.

Poultry and Game

Poultry and game cook beautifully in the crockpot, as little liquid is needed for casseroles and a rich flavour is preserved during slow cooking. It is very important that frozen birds or game animals should be completely thawed before cooking in a crockpot, and it is not advisable to stuff the birds as the heat may not penetrate the stuffing completely. Birds must be roasted on the HIGH setting, and it is advisable to casserole birds on the HIGH setting for at least 30 minutes, before switching to LOW for slow cooking.

Small whole birds (3–4 lb/1·5–2 kg) may be cooked, but poultry joints are particularly suitable for crockpot cooking. Poultry does not take as long as other meat to cook, but the principles of preparation for crockpot cookery remain the same. Root vegetables are best arranged on the bottom of the crockpot with the poultry or game on top and the liquid poured over. As with meat, the flavour and appearance of poultry and game are improved if sealed in hot fat before putting into the crockpot. It is possible simply to put vegetables, chicken or rabbit joints and liquid into the crockpot and cook them without preparation, but the result can be dull. A few minutes spent on pre-cooking makes all the difference, and so does the addition of strongly-flavoured ingredients such as tomatoes, garlic, herbs and spices, and fruit. Duck can be cooked in many ways too, but releases a good deal of fat and, as will be seen from the recipes, it is advisable to remove excess fat towards the end of cooking time.

Roast Chicken

3 lb/1.5 kg chicken
2 oz/50 g butter
2 tablespoons/30 ml oil
Salt and pepper

Wipe the chicken well and season inside and out. Brown on all sides in the butter and oil. Grease the crockpot lightly and put in the chicken. Cover and cook on HIGH for 5–6 hours. It is most important that frozen birds should be completely thawed, drained and wiped before use. It is not advisable to stuff a chicken before roasting in the crockpot. A chicken up to 4 lb/ 2 kg may be roasted in this way, and will need 6–7 hours on HIGH. Chicken joints may be cooked in the same way, cooking on HIGH for 30 minutes, and then on LOW for 3 hours.

Poached Chicken

3 lb/1.5 kg chicken
Salt and pepper
1 celery stick
1 medium carrot
1 medium onion
1 bayleaf
1 sprig parsley
1 sprig thyme
½ pint/300 ml water
Salt and pepper

Remove the giblets from the chicken and clean them. Put the chicken and the giblets into the crockpot. Chop the vegetables finely and put them round the chicken. Place the herbs on top and add boiling water and seasoning. Cover and cook on HIGH for 1 hour, then on LOW for 7–8 hours. Lift out the chicken and leave until cold. Use the chicken flesh for all kinds of cold dishes, or for making pies, meat loaves, etc. Strain the chicken stock into a bowl and leave until cold and jellied. Take off any fat, and use stock for soups or casserole dishes.

Lemon Herb Chicken

3 lb/1.5 kg chicken
Salt and pepper
1 garlic clove
1 teaspoon marjoram
2 oz/50 g butter
2 tablespoons/30 ml oil
Juice of 1 lemon
¼ pint/300 ml chicken stock

Wipe the chicken and season inside and out with salt and pepper. Put the chopped garlic and marjoram inside the chicken. Brown the chicken in butter and oil and put into the crockpot. Add the lemon juice and chicken stock. Cover and cook on HIGH for 2 hours, then on LOW for 6–7 hours. Try serving this with new potatoes and peas or broad beans. Rosemary may be used instead of marjoram.

Chicken Casserole

4–6 chicken joints
2 oz/50 g lard
1 medium carrot
1 medium onion
2 celery sticks
2 tomatoes
1 oz/25 g plain flour
Pinch of mixed herbs
Salt and pepper
1 pint/500 ml water or stock

Wipe the chicken pieces and cook them in the lard until golden. Lift out the chicken pieces and keep on one side. Chop the carrot, onion and celery finely and cook in the fat until the onion is soft and golden. Put the vegetables into the crockpot and put the chicken pieces on top. Peel the tomatoes and remove the pips. Cut the flesh into pieces and add to the crockpot. Stir the flour into the fat and pan juices and cook for 2 minutes. Add the herbs, seasoning and stock and bring to the boil. Pour over the chicken, cover and cook on HIGH for 30 minutes, then on LOW for 7–8 hours.

Cider Chicken

4–6 chicken joints
2 oz/50 g butter
2 tablespoons/30 ml oil
1 medium onion
½ pint/300 ml dry cider
3 tablespoons/45 ml brandy
Salt and pepper
2 cooking apples
8 oz/225 g button mushrooms
1 oz/25 g butter
1 oz/25 g plain flour

Wipe the chicken joints. Brown them on all sides in the butter and oil, and put into the crockpot. Add the finely chopped onion, cider and brandy, and season well. Cover and cook on HIGH for 30 minutes, then on LOW for 4–5 hours. Add the peeled and sliced apples, and the mushrooms cut in half. Work together the butter and flour into a paste and stir into the crockpot. Cover and continue cooking for 2–3 hours.

Chicken in Red Wine

4–6 chicken joints
2 oz/50 g lard
4 oz/100 g streaky bacon
1 large onion
1 garlic clove
4 oz/100 g button mushrooms
2 oz/50 g flour
Salt and pepper
1 bayleaf
Sprig of parsley
Sprig of thyme
2 cloves
½ pint/300 ml red wine
½ pint/300 ml chicken stock

Cook the chicken pieces in the lard until golden. Lift out of the fat and put the chicken into the crockpot. Chop the bacon and onion finely and crush the garlic. Cook in the fat left from the chicken until the onion is soft and golden. Drain and sprinkle on the chicken, together with the small whole mushrooms. Stir the flour into the pan juices and cook for 2 minutes. Add the seasoning, herbs, cloves, wine and stock and bring to the boil. Pour over the chicken, cover and cook on HIGH for 30 minutes, then on LOW for 7–8 hours. Garnish with some freshly chopped parsley before serving.

Chicken in White Wine

4–6 chicken joints
3 tablespoons/45 ml oil
1 medium onion
2 medium carrots
3 celery sticks
Salt and pepper
Pinch of basil
¼ pint/300 ml dry white wine
¼ pint/300 ml chicken stock

Wipe the chicken joints and cook in the oil until golden. Drain from the oil and keep on one side. Chop the onion, carrots and celery finely and cook in the oil until the onion is soft and golden. Put the vegetables in the crockpot and put in the chicken joints. Season with salt, pepper and basil. Mix together the wine and stock and pour over the chicken. Cover and cook on HIGH for 30 minutes and then on LOW for 7–8 hours.

Chicken with Grapes

4–6 chicken joints
2 oz/50 g butter
2 tablespoons/30 ml oil
1 teaspoon tarragon
¼ pint/150 ml chicken stock
4 tablespoons/60 ml dry white wine
Salt and pepper
8 oz/225 g seedless grapes
4 tablespoons/60 ml double cream

Wipe the chicken joints. Brown them on all sides in the butter and oil, and put into the crockpot. Add the terragon, chicken stock, wine and seasoning. Cover and cook on HIGH for 30 minutes, then on LOW for 6–7 hours. Thirty minutes before serving, stir in the grapes and cream and continue cooking. If seedless grapes are not obtainable, use white grapes which have been peeled and seeded.

Chicken and Pineapple

4–6 chicken joints
Salt and pepper
2 oz/50 g butter
2 tablespoons/30 ml oil
¼ pint/150 ml chicken stock
8 oz/225 g canned crushed pineapple
1 cooking apple
1 oz/25 g soft brown sugar
2 tablespoons/30 ml dry sherry

Wipe the chicken joints. Season with salt and pepper and brown the chicken on all sides in the butter and oil. Drain and put into the crockpot. Add the chicken stock and drained pineapple (if canned crushed pineapple is not available. use pineapple chunks broken with a fork or shredded in a blender). Add the peeled and sliced apple, sugar, sherry and additional seasoning. Cover and cook on HIGH for 30 minutes, then on LOW for 6–7 hours. This is very good with rice and a green salad.

Chicken in Barbecue Sauce

1½ oz/40 g butter
2 tablespoons/30 ml oil
3 lb/1.5 kg chicken
Salt and pepper
1 small onion
4 tablespoons/60 ml tomato sauce
2 tablespoons/30 ml vinegar
2 tablespoons/30 ml chutney
½ teaspoon French mustard
1 teaspoon caster sugar
1 tablespoon/15 ml Worcestershire sauce

Rub the inside of the crockpot with a little of the butter. Put the remaining butter and oil in a thick pan. Wipe the chicken and season inside and out with salt and pepper. Heat the butter and oil and brown the chicken all over. Put into the crockpot. Chop the onion finely and cook it in the fat until soft and golden. Add the tomato sauce, vinegar, chopped chutney, mustard, sugar and Worcestershire sauce and bring to the boil. Pour over the chicken and cook on HIGH for 30 minutes, then on LOW for 7–8 hours basting the chicken with the sauce once or twice.

Chicken in Curry Sauce

4–6 chicken joints
Pinch of salt
2 tablespoons/30 ml oil
2 medium onions
½ oz/15 g curry powder
½ oz/15 g plain flour
½ pint/300 ml chicken stock
1 tablespoon/15 ml vinegar
½ oz/15 g sugar
1 tablespoon/15 ml apricot jam
1 oz/25 g sultanas

Put the chicken joints into a saucepan, cover with hot water and add salt, and simmer until the chicken is tender. Drain off the liquid and keep it in reserve. Remove the meat from the chicken joints in large pieces. Slice the onions thinly and cook in the oil until soft and golden. Stir in the curry powder and flour and cook for 2 minutes, stirring well. Measure the reserved chicken stock and add to the onions. Stir well and heat gently until the sauce is smooth. Add the vinegar, sugar, jam and sultanas. Put the chicken pieces into the crockpot, pour over the curry sauce and stir well. Cover and cook on HIGH for 30 minutes, then on LOW for 4–5 hours.

Chicken Niçoise

4–6 chicken joints
3 tablespoons/45 ml oil
1 oz/25 g butter
2 medium onions
3 garlic cloves
8 oz/225 g mushrooms
Pinch of basil
¼ pint/300 ml dry white wine
1 lb/450 g canned tomatoes
Salt and pepper
12 black olives
4 tablespoons/60 ml chopped parsley

Wipe the chicken joints and cook in the oil and butter until golden on all sides. Lift out of fat and keep on one side. Slice the onions finely, chop the cloves and slice the mushrooms. Cook in the remaining fat until the onions are soft and golden. Drain the vegetables and put into the crockpot with the chicken joints on top. Add the basil and wine to the fat and heat until the wine is reduced by half. Pour this mixture over the chicken. Add the drained tomatoes, salt and pepper, and olives and sprinkle parsley on top. Cover and cook on HIGH for 30 minutes, then on LOW for 7–8 hours.

Spanish Chicken

4–6 chicken joints
2 oz/50 g butter
1 tablespoon/15 ml oil
1 streaky bacon rasher
1 medium onion
2 oz/50 g plain flour
1 pint/500 ml chicken stock
1 medium carrot
4 oz/100 g tomato purée
1 bayleaf
Sprig of parsley
Sprig of thyme
1 slice green pepper
4 oz/100 g button mushrooms
Salt and pepper
3 tablespoons/45 ml sherry

Wipe the chicken joints and cook in the butter and oil until golden on all sides. Lift from the fat and put into the crockpot. Chop the bacon and onion finely and cook in the remaining fat until the onion is soft and golden. Stir in the flour and add the stock slowly. Bring to the boil, stirring well. Add the finely sliced carrot, tomato purée, herbs, chopped green pepper, sliced mushrooms and seasoning, and pour over the chicken. Cover and cook on HIGH for 30 minutes, then on LOW for 7–8 hours. Take out the bayleaf, parsley and thyme and stir in the sherry. Continue cooking on LOW for 30 minutes.

Moroccan Chicken

4–6 chicken joints
2 tablespoons/30 ml oil
1 oz/25 g butter
1 large onion
1 teaspoon ground ginger
2 teaspoons paprika
½ teaspoon turmeric
Salt and pepper
1 tablespoon/15 ml lemon juice
½ pint/300 ml chicken stock
12 stuffed olives
1 lemon

Wipe the chicken joints. Cook in the oil and butter until golden on all sides. Drain and keep on one side. Slice the onion thinly and cook in the fat until soft and golden. Put the onion into the crockpot and put the chicken joints on top. Mix the spices, salt and pepper with the lemon juice and spread on the chicken joints. Pour on the chicken stock, cover and cook on HIGH for 30 minutes, then on LOW for 7–8 hours. Cut the olives in slices and cut the lemon in slices without peeling. Put on top of the chicken and cook on HIGH for 15 minutes just before serving.

African Chicken

4–6 chicken joints
3 tablespoons/45 ml oil
2 medium onions
2 large tomatoes
½ pint/300 ml chicken stock
2 garlic cloves
4 oz/100 g chunky peanut butter
2 teaspoons ground chili spice
Salt and pepper
1 green pepper
2 oz/50 g salted peanuts

Wipe the joints and cook in the oil until golden. Remove from the oil and keep on one side. Chop the onions finely, cook in the oil until soft and golden and put into the crockpot. Place the chicken joints on the onions. Peel the tomatoes, remove the pips, and cut the flesh into pieces. Put the tomatoes, chicken stock, crushed garlic, peanut butter, chili spice, salt and pepper into the crockpot. Cover and cook on HIGH for 30 minutes, then on LOW for 7–8 hours. Chop the green pepper finely, mix with the salted peanuts, and sprinkle on the surface of the chicken before serving with rice.

Paprika Chicken

4–6 chicken joints
Salt and pepper
2 oz/50 g butter
2 tablespoons/30 ml oil
½ oz/15 g paprika
2 medium onions
1 green or red pepper
2 tomatoes
¼ pint/150 ml chicken stock
1 teaspoon vinegar
½ oz/15 g butter
½ oz/15 g plain flour
¼ pint/150 ml commercial soured cream

Wipe the chicken joints, season well, and brown on all sides in the butter and oil. Put into the crockpot with paprika, finely sliced onions and pepper. Peel the tomatoes, remove the pips, and cut the flesh into strips. Put into the crockpot with the vinegar. Cover and cook on HIGH for 30 minutes, then on LOW for 4–5 hours. Work together the butter and flour into a paste and stir into the crockpot. Cover and continue cooking for 2–3 hours. Just before serving, stir in the soured cream.

Chinese Chicken

1 tablespoon/15 ml oil
4–6 chicken joints
2 large onions
1 oz/25 g cornflour
¼ pint/150 ml chicken stock
12 oz/350 g button mushrooms
2 tablespoons/30 ml soy sauce
Juice of 1 lemon
1 teaspoon sugar
Salt and pepper

Heat the oil and fry on all sides, until golden. Take out the chicken and put into the crockpot. Chop the onions finely and cook in the oil until soft and golden. Mix the cornflour with a little of the cold stock. Stir in the remaining stock and then add to the onions. Add the mushrooms cut in half, soy sauce, lemon juice, sugar, salt and pepper, and bring to the boil. Pour over the chicken and cook on HIGH for 30 minutes, then on LOW for 7–8 hours.

Sweet and Sour Chicken

4–6 chicken joints
1 tablespoon/15 ml Worcestershire sauce
1 tablespoon/15 ml soy sauce
Pinch of pepper
1 teaspoon sugar
1 garlic clove
2 tablespoons/30 ml oil
8 oz/225 g pineapple chunks
½ pint/300 ml chicken stock
1 teaspoon/5 ml vinegar
½ oz/15 g cornflour

Wipe the chicken joints. Mix the Worcestershire sauce, soy sauce, pepper and sugar and brush the chicken joints with this mixture. Chop the garlic and fry in the oil until golden. Add the chicken and fry for 10 minutes until golden on all sides. Put the chicken into the crockpot and add the pineapple cut into small pieces, chicken stock and vinegar. Cover and cook on HIGH for 30 minutes and then on LOW for 7–8 hours. An hour before serving time, mix the cornflour with a little water and stir into the sauce, and continue cooking. Serve with rice or noodles.

Duck Casserole

4 lb/2 kg duck
Salt and pepper
1 tablespoon/15 ml oil
1 oz/25 g butter
1 medium onion
1 celery stick
1 bayleaf
8 oz/225 g mushrooms
½ pint/300 ml chicken stock
¼ pint/150 ml dry white wine

Wipe the duck and cut into four quarters. Prick well with a fork and season with salt and pepper. Cook in the oil and butter until golden on all sides. Drain and keep on one side. Chop the onion and celery finely and cook in the fat until the onion is soft and golden. Put the vegetables into the crockpot and put the duck pieces on top, seasoning well, and adding the bayleaf. Slice the mushrooms and cook in the remaining fat. Drain and put on to the duck pieces. Pour over the stock and wine, cover and cook on HIGH for 30 minutes, then on LOW for 7–8 hours.

Duck in Red Wine

4 lb/2 kg duck
1 garlic clove
1 medium onion
Pinch of nutmeg
Pinch of salt
4 tablespoons/60 ml brandy
½ pint/300 ml red wine
4 tablespoons/60 ml orange juice
2 oz/50 g butter
2 tablespoons/30 ml oil
1 bayleaf

Cut the duck into pieces and make short cuts in the skin with
a sharp knife. Crush the garlic and mix with finely chopped
onion, nutmeg, salt, brandy, wine and orange juice. Put the
duck pieces into a bowl and pour over the mixture. Leave in
the refrigerator overnight. Drain the duck and brown on all
sides in the butter and oil. Put into the crockpot, pour over the
wine mixture and add the bayleaf. Cover and cook on HIGH
for 1 hour, then on LOW for 7–8 hours. Take off any surplus
fat before serving.

Summer Duck

4 lb/2 kg duck
2 oz/50 g butter
2 tablespoons/30 ml oil
4 streaky bacon rashers
12 small onions (pickling size)
½ oz/15 g flour
½ pint/300 ml stock
1 lb/450 g shelled peas
4 lettuce leaves
1 bayleaf
1 sprig parsley
1 sprig thyme
Salt and pepper

Wipe the duck and season inside and out. Brown all over in the butter and oil and put into the crockpot. Chop the bacon finely and cook in the fat until golden. Peel the small onions and cook whole until golden. Put bacon and onions round the duck. Mix the flour with the remaining fat and cook for 2 minutes. Stir in the stock and cook for 5 minutes. Pour over the duck, cover and cook on HIGH for 30 minutes, then on LOW for 6 hours. Drain off any surplus fat, and add the peas, lettuce leaves, herbs and seasoning to the crockpot. Cover and continue cooking on LOW for 2 hours. Arrange the duck on a serving dish and surround with the peas. Strain the gravy, reheat and serve with the duck.

Duck in Port

4 lb/2 kg duck
1 tablespoon/15 ml oil
2 medium onions
3 sage leaves
Salt and pepper
¼ pint/150 ml giblet stock
¼ pint/150 ml port
1 lemon

Wipe the duck and season inside and out with salt and pepper. Heat the oil and brown the duck on all sides. Put into the crockpot, cover and cook on LOW for 7 hours. Drain off the duck fat. In the fat left from browning the duck, cook the finely chopped onions until soft and golden. Add the chopped sage leaves, salt and pepper. Put these round the duck and pour over the stock and port. Continue cooking on LOW for 2 hours, and add the juice of the lemon just before serving. A garnish of fried bread triangles is good with this dish. The giblet stock should be made by simmering the duck giblets (without the liver) in a little water to make a rich gravy.

Duck in Orange Sauce

4 lb/2 kg duck
Salt and pepper
1 tablespoon/15 ml oil
1 oz/15 g butter
2 medium onions
1 oz/25 g plain flour
¾ pint/400 ml orange juice

Wipe the duck and season inside and out with salt and pepper. Heat the oil and brown the duck on all sides. Put into the crockpot, cover and cook on HIGH for 30 minutes, then on LOW for 7 hours. Drain off the duck fat. In the fat left from browning the duck, cook the finely chopped onions until soft and golden. Add the flour and cook for 2 minutes. Stir in the orange juice and pour over the duck. Cook on LOW for 2 hours.

Rabbit with Dumplings

1 rabbit
1 large onion
1 oz/25 g lard
1 oz/25 g plain flour
½ pint/300 ml chicken stock
2 tablespoons/30 ml Worcestershire sauce
Salt and pepper

Dumplings
4 oz/100 g self-raising flour
2 oz/50 g shredded suet
Salt and pepper
3 tablespoons/45 ml water

Cut the rabbit into joints and put into a pan of cold water. Bring to the boil, boil for 2 minutes and drain the rabbit joints. Chop the onion finely and fry in the lard until soft and golden. Drain and put into the crockpot. Coat the rabbit joints in flour and cook in the fat until golden. Put on top of the onion. Add the stock, Worcestershire sauce, salt and pepper to the pan juices and stir over heat until boiling. Pour over the rabbit and cook on HIGH for 30 minutes, then on LOW for 6–9 hours.

Make the dumplings by mixing together the sifted flour, suet, seasoning and water and making into six balls. Put into the crockpot and cook on HIGH for 45 minutes.

Jugged Rabbit

1 rabbit
4 oz/100 g fresh white breadcrumbs
½ oz/15 g mixed herbs
8 oz/225 g cooking apples
2 small onions
Salt and pepper
6 cloves
Juice of 1 lemon
1 pint/500 ml water

Cut the rabbit into joints and put into a pan of cold water.
Bring to the boil, boil for 2 minutes and drain the rabbit joints.
Put the rabbit into the crockpot and cover with the breadcrumbs, herbs and finely chopped apples and onions, seasoning
well. Put in the cloves and add the lemon juice and water.
Cover and cook on HIGH for 30 minutes, then on LOW for
6–8 hours. Remove the cloves before serving.

Rabbit Casserole

1 rabbit
1 onion
2 tomatoes
Salt and pepper
Pinch of mixed herbs
1 pint/500 ml water

Cut the rabbit into joints and put into a pan of cold water. Bring to the boil, boil for 2 minutes and drain the rabbit joints. Chop the onion finely and put into the crockpot. Put the rabbit joints on top. Peel the tomatoes, remove the pips, and cut flesh in pieces. Put on top of the rabbit joints with the seasoning, herbs and water. Cover and cook on HIGH for 30 minutes, then on LOW for 6–8 hours. This is very good if cider is substituted for half the water. If thick gravy is liked, a little flour may be blended with water and then stirred into the casserole an hour before serving time.

Pigeon and Mushroom Casserole

2 pigeons
8 oz/225 g chuck steak
1 streaky bacon rasher
2 tablespoons/30 ml oil
1 oz/25 g butter
2 oz/50 g mushrooms
Salt and pepper
1 tablespoon/15 ml redcurrant jelly
1 tablespoon/15 ml lemon juice
½ pint/300 ml beef stock
½ oz/15 g plain flour

Cut the pigeons in half and the steak in small cubes. Chop the
bacon finely. Put the bacon in a heavy pan and cook until the
fat runs. Add the oil and butter and cook the pigeons and steak
until the surfaces are sealed. Put the steak, bacon and pigeons
into the crockpot and cover with the sliced mushrooms. Season
and add the redcurrant jelly, lemon juice and stock. Cover and
cook on HIGH for 30 minutes and then on LOW for 7–8
hours. About 45 minutes before serving time, mix the flour
with a little water and stir into the gravy. Continue cooking
until serving time.

Somerset Pigeons

2 pigeons
1 large onion
2 celery sticks
1 lb/450 g eating apples
Salt and pepper
Pinch of paprika
Pinch of nutmeg
½ pint/300 ml dry cider
1 teaspoon Worcestershire sauce

Wipe the pigeons and split them in half down the breastbone.
Slice the onion thinly and put into the crockpot. Chop the
celery and add to the onions. Peel the apples and cut in thin
slices. Put into the casserole and top with the pigeon halves.
Season with salt and pepper, paprika and nutmeg and pour
over the cider and Worcestershire sauce. Cover and cook on
HIGH for 30 minutes and then on LOW for 7–8 hours.

Braised Pigeons

2 pigeons
2 medium onions
4 oz/125 g fresh white breadcrumbs
1 teaspoon sage
Salt and pepper
1 oz/25 g butter
2 tablespoons/30 ml milk
2 tablespoons/30 ml oil
4 oz/100 g mushrooms
3 oz/75 g streaky bacon
½ oz/15 g plain flour
1 pint/500 ml chicken stock

Wipe the pigeons and season inside and out with salt and pepper. Chop one of the onions finely and cook in a little boiling water until tender. Drain and mix with the breadcrumbs, sage, salt and pepper, butter and milk. Stuff the pigeons with the mixture. Heat the oil and fry the pigeons until golden brown on all sides. Put into the crockpot. Chop the mushrooms and bacon and remaining onion, and cook in the oil until the onion is soft and golden. Stir in the flour and add the stock slowly. Bring to the boil, season with salt and pepper and pour over the pigeons. Cover and cook on HIGH for 30 minutes, then on LOW for 7–8 hours. To serve, split the pigeons in half down the breastbone and serve each half with a portion of stuffing and the sauce from the crockpot.

Pheasant in Cider

1 pheasant
6 oz/150 g small pickling onions
2 oz/50 g butter
1 lb/450 g cooking apples
1 garlic clove
1 tablespoon/15 ml black treacle
½ pint/300 ml cider
Salt and pepper

Wipe the pheasant and season inside and out with salt and pepper. Peel the onions and cook them in the butter until golden. Put the onions into the crockpot and put the pheasant on top. Peel the apples and cut them in eighths. Put round the pheasant with the crushed garlic, treacle, cider and seasoning. Cover and cook on HIGH for 30 minutes, then on LOW for 8–9 hours. The pheasant may be served straight from the crockpot, but if liked the apples and liquid in the dish may be sieved and poured over the pheasant before serving.

Partridge and Mushrooms

2 partridges
12 oz/350 g mushrooms
2 tablespoons/30 ml oil
3 oz/75 g butter
½ pint/300 ml chicken stock
4 tablespoons/60 ml sherry
Salt and pepper

Wipe the partridges. Slice the mushrooms and cook them in two-thirds of the butter until tender. Season the mushrooms and put half of them on one side. Stuff the partridges with the remaining mushrooms and brown the partridges on all sides in the oil and remaining butter. Put the partridges into the crockpot and pour over the chicken stock and sherry. Cover and cook on HIGH for 30 minutes, then on LOW for 7–8 hours. About 45 minutes before serving time, stir in the remaining mushrooms and continue cooking. The gravy is rich and delicious, but if a thick gravy is preferred, a little flour mixed with water may be added to the crockpot with the additional mushrooms.

Harvest Partridge

2 partridges
2 tablespoons/30 ml oil
1 oz/25 g butter
1 small onion
2 oz/50 g button mushrooms
8 oz/225 g courgettes
Salt and pepper
¼ pint/300 ml red wine
½ oz/15 g plain flour

Wipe the partridges and season inside and out with salt and pepper. Cook them in oil and butter until browned on all sides. Take the partridges out of the fat and keep on one side. Chop the onion finely, keep the mushrooms whole, and slice the courgettes without peeling. Cook them in the oil until the onion is soft and golden, and then put the vegetables into the crockpot. Put the partridges on top. Season and add the wine. Cover and cook on HIGH for 30 minutes, then on LOW for 7–8 hours. About 45 minutes before serving, mix the flour with a little cold water and then stir into the liquid in the crockpot, and baste the partridges. Continue cooking until serving time.

Jugged Hare and Forcemeat Balls

1 hare
Salt and pepper
2 oz/50 g lard
1 medium onion
1 tablespoon/15 ml lemon juice
1 teaspoon sugar
½ pint/300 ml port
1 bayleaf
Pinch of ground mace
Sprig of parsley
½ oz/15 g plain flour
2 tablespoons/30 ml redcurrant jelly

Forcemeat Balls
4 oz/100 g fresh white breadcrumbs
2 oz/50 g suet
1 tablespoon chopped parsley
1 teaspoon mixed herbs
Salt and pepper
1 beaten egg

Since a hare is rather a large animal, it may not be possible to cook all the pieces in one of the smaller crockpots. In this case, use enough pieces as you need and cook the rest of the hare as pâté or soup. You need not alter the other ingredients. Cut the hare into joints and season with salt and pepper. Cut the onion in thin slices. Cook the hare and onion in the fat until the hare is lightly browned. Put into the crockpot with the lemon juice, sugar, port, bayleaf, mace and parsley. Cover and cook on LOW for 10–11 hours. About 45 minutes before serving time, mix the flour with a little cold water and add to the crockpot with the redcurrant jelly and any blood drained from the hare when it was first hung. Add the prepared forcemeat balls, cover and continue cooking until serving time.

To make the forcemeat balls, rub the breadcrumbs finely and mix with the suet, parsley, herbs, seasoning and enough beaten egg to bind. Shape the mixture into small balls and fry them in a little butter before adding to the crockpot.

Venison Casserole

2 lb/1 kg venison
4 oz/100 g streaky bacon
2 medium onions
1 pint/500 ml dry cider
4 tablespoons/60 ml cranberry sauce
2 cloves
1 bayleaf
Pinch of thyme
Salt and pepper

Cut the venison in small cubes. Chop the bacon and put into a
heavy pan. Heat gently until the fat runs and then brown the
pieces of venison with the bacon. Lift out the pieces of bacon
and venison and put into the crockpot. Chop the onions finely
and cook in the fat until golden and soft. Add to the crockpot
with the cider, cranberry sauce, cloves, bayleaf, thyme, salt and
pepper. Cover and cook on LOW for 8–10 hours. Venison can
often be bought from country butchers and from freezer centres.
It is a lean meat and rather dry and is better-flavoured and tex-
tured if left to soak in cider or wine for some hours before
cooking. If there is time to spare, cut up the venison and leave
overnight in the cider with herbs and spices. The venison
should then be drained and browned in the fat before being put
in the crockpot. The liquid in which it has been marinaded or
soaked can then be used for cooking.

Meat

All kinds of meat and offal can be cooked in the crockpot, and the long slow cooking is particularly suitable for cheaper, less tender cuts which benefit from being sealed in the moistness of the crockpot at a low temperature. Any liquid in the dish becomes full of flavour and no food value is lost during slow cooking. Traditional casserole recipes may be used, but preparation for crockpot cookery differs in one or two small details.

Preparation Methods

Oddly enough, vegetables take longer to cook than meat in a crockpot. For this reason, such vegetables as carrots, turnips or celery should be cut in thin slices or small chunks and put on the bottom and round the sides of the crockpot before the meat is added. Since juices do not evaporate from the crockpot, the quantity of liquid in a recipe will be smaller than for conventional methods. This liquid may be water, stock, tomato juice or liquid from a can, cider or beer, and generally the amount for a family-sized stew will be about ½ pint/300 ml – a little more is generally allowed if potatoes or rice are in the recipe since they absorb liquid during cooking.

It is possible to prepare many casseroles by 'one-step cookery' in the crockpot, simply putting in layers of vegetables, meat and flavouring herbs or spices, plus liquid. While this is a quick and easy method of cooking, it does result in a rather 'stewed' taste and ragged meat. I prefer to seal meat in a little fat before adding to the crockpot, and usually to cook lightly such additions as onions and bacon, which results in an improved texture and far better flavour. Fat meats such as pork may be browned without additional fat, and surplus fat can then be drained off, again resulting in a better finish for a dish.

If meat is lightly tossed in flour before frying, this will result in a slightly thickened gravy. The addition of tomato purée or vegetable purée or the use of potatoes or rice will also give thickness. A little flour may be stirred into the frying fat, then browned and cooked for a few minutes with the liquid in the recipe before adding to the crockpot for a rich gravy. If you prefer to adjust the thickness of the gravy nearer serving time, there are a number of ways to do this. A small ball of butter and flour can be added to the crockpot and the temperature raised to HIGH for 30 minutes before serving. Thickening can also be achieved by mixing a little flour and water to a smooth paste before adding to the crockpot, but use cornflour for Chinese-style dishes to give the correct texture. Commercial soured cream, single or double cream is also used in some recipes to thicken and flavour sauces, but these should only be stirred in just before serving time.

Flavours are intensified in the crockpot as there is no evaporation of liquid. The recipes in this book have been prepared to allow for this, but if you want to adapt conventional recipes you will find you need less of the stronger flavoured vegetables such as onions and turnips, and also of herbs and spices.

Cooking Times

A wide variation in cooking times may be seen in the recipes. Until you are used to your crockpot, test meat and vegetables after the minimum cooking time to see if they are to your taste. The thickness of the pieces can affect cooking time, and bones will conduct heat more quickly through the meat. There can also be slight variations in current supply during a day which may result in fluctuating temperatures occasionally. As the cooking temperature is so low, dishes will not suffer for being left for an hour or two longer, and there is no danger of sticking or burning. After one or two experiments, you will quickly judge the cooking time which best suits your taste.

Most recipes for the crockpot are suitable for very long cooking on LOW, which makes them suitable for an evening meal which can be started early in the day. For a midday meal, use HIGH setting for just over half the time required for all-day cooking. Check with the manufacturer's instructions to see if the crockpot should be pre-heated before ingredients are put in as this is recommended for some types. I always prefer to cook on HIGH setting for at least 30 minutes before switching to LOW, but again the manufacturer's instructions should be followed. Some cookers need no pre-heating or HIGH cooking before all-day slow cooking, while others recommend an hour or two on the higher setting before reducing the temperature and this can be inconvenient for someone who is out all day and wants the crockpot to work without fuss. When adding dumplings or thickening gravy, switch the cooker to HIGH to finish the dish. For your first experiments with the crockpot, choose a recipe from this book and then find a similar specimen in your manufacturer's booklet which will give you general guidance about using your particular model.

Roasting
Particular care should be taken about roasting meat in a crockpot, which is not recommended for some types. Depending on the size of the container, joints from 3–5 lb/1·5–2·5 kg in weight may be roasted, depending on the shape of the joint. Suitable joints are shoulder or half-leg of lamb, shoulder of pork and topside of beef. Before cooking, the meat should be well-seasoned and browned on all sides in a separate pan. Cooking time on HIGH, which is recommended for all roasting, will take from 4–6 hours, allowing the maximum time for pork. Pork rind should be removed before cooking, but other joints need no special preparation. Meat juices will collect in the crockpot which make excellent gravy. If you like a crisp finish to the joint, it may be transferred to another dish and browned in a hot oven for the last 30 minutes of cooking time – if your crockpot has a separate stoneware pot, this may be put into the oven for the browning process.

Beef Casserole

1½ lb/700 g stewing steak
1 oz/25 g plain flour
Salt and pepper
2 tablespoons/30 ml cooking oil
2 large onions
3 medium carrots
1 pint/500 ml beef stock

Cut the steak into 1 in./2·5 cm cubes and toss in the flour seasoned with salt and pepper. Brown on all sides in the oil, then remove from the pan. Cut the onions in thin slices and cook in the oil until soft and golden. Slice the carrots thinly and put into the crockpot. Top with the onions and the meat. Add any remaining flour to the fat in the pan and cook for 2 minutes. Work in the stock and stir over low heat until the liquid comes to the boil. Pour into the crockpot, cover and cook on HIGH for 30 minutes, then on LOW for 6–7 hours.

Steak and Kidney Casserole

1 lb/450 g stewing steak
4 oz/100 g ox kidney
1 oz/25 g plain flour
Salt and pepper
1 small onion
1 oz/25 g lard
¾ pint/400 ml water

Cut the steak and kidney into 1 in./2·5 cm cubes and toss in the flour seasoned with salt and pepper. Brown on all sides in the hot lard. Chop the onion finely and cook in the fat until soft and golden. Add the water and stir well, bringing to the boil. Put into the crockpot, cover and cook in HIGH for 30 minutes, then on LOW for 6–7 hours. A few sliced mushrooms may be added with the onions if liked. This casserole may be eaten sprinkled with plenty of chopped parsley, or used as the filling for a pie. If you are using a crockpot with stoneware lining, the dish may be lifted out, covered with pastry and baked at 200 °C/400 °F/Gas Mark 6 for 40 minutes.

Spiced Beef and Beans

2 lb/1 kg stewing steak
1 oz/25 g plain flour
Salt and pepper
Pinch of ground ginger
2 oz/50 g lard
8 oz/225 canned tomatoes
4 oz/100 g mushrooms
1 green or red pepper
Few drops of Tabasco sauce
1 tablespoon/15 ml Worcestershire sauce
1 oz/25 g soft brown sugar
2 tablespoons/30 ml wine vinegar
2 garlic cloves
1 bayleaf
1 lb/450 g canned kidney beans

Cut the steak into 1 in./2·5 cm cubes. Toss the meat in the flour mixed with salt, pepper and ginger. Brown the meat on all sides in the lard and then put into the crockpot. Put the tomatoes and their juice, sliced mushrooms and pepper, Tabasco and Worcestershire sauces, sugar, vinegar, crushed garlic and bayleaf into the pan and bring to the boil. Pour over the meat and cover. Cook on HIGH for 30 minutes, then on LOW for 6–7 hours. Drain the kidney beans, add to the crockpot and continue cooking for 30 minutes. Take out the bayleaf before serving.

Beef or Pork Goulash

1½ lb/700 g stewing steak *or* lean pork
1 oz/25 g plain flour
Salt and pepper
2 tablespoons/30 ml oil
2 large onions
1 green pepper
¼ pint/150 ml beef stock
1 lb/450 g canned tomatoes
2 teaspoons/10 ml paprika
2 tablespoons/30 ml tomato purée
1 bayleaf
Sprig of parsley
Sprig of thyme
4 tablespoons/60 ml commercial soured cream

Cut the meat into 1 in/2·5 cm cubes and toss in flour seasoned with salt and pepper. Brown the meat in the oil and then add the thinly sliced onions and pepper, and cook until soft and golden. Add the stock, the tomatoes including their juice, paprika, tomato purée and herbs. Season to taste, stir and bring to the boil. Pour into the crockpot, cover and cook on HIGH for 30 minutes, then on LOW for 6–7 hours. Stir in the soured cream just before serving.

Burgundy Beef

2 lb/1 kg stewing steak
2 tablespoons/30 ml oil
4 oz/100 g streaky bacon rashers
1 oz/25 g plain flour
¼ pint/150 ml red wine
2 tablespoons/30 ml brandy
Pinch of thyme
1 bayleaf
1 garlic clove
10 small onions (pickling size)
Salt and pepper

Cut the steak into 1 in./2·5 cm cubes. Brown on all sides in the oil. Put the meat into the crockpot. Chop the bacon and cook it in the oil until just cooked but not crisp. Stir in the flour and cook for 2 minutes. Add the wine, brandy, herbs, crushed garlic and peeled whole onions. Stir well and bring to the boil. Pour over the meat and season well. Cover and cook on HIGH for 30 minutes, then on LOW for 6–7 hours. Take out the bayleaf before serving.

Curried Beef

2 lb/1 kg stewing steak
2 oz/50 g lard
2 large onions
1 large cooking apple
½ oz/15 g curry powder
1 oz/25 g plain flour
¾ pint/400 ml beef stock
2 oz/50 g sultanas
4 tomatoes
2 tablespoons/30 ml chutney
Juice of ½ lemon
Salt and pepper

Cut the steak into 1 in./2.5 cm cubes. Brown on all sides in the lard. Put the meat into the crockpot. Chop the onions and cook in the fat until soft and golden. Add the peeled and chopped apple and cook for 3 minutes. Stir in the curry powder and cook for 2 minutes. Work in the flour and then the stock, and bring to the boil, stirring all the time. Pour over the meat in the crockpot. Add the sultanas. Peel the tomatoes, remove the pips, and cut the flesh into pieces. Add to the crockpot with the chutney, lemon juice and seasoning. Cover and cook on HIGH for 30 minutes, then on LOW for 6–7 hours. Serve with boiled rice and chutney.

Stuffed Beef Rolls

1 lb/450 g braising steak
2 oz/50 g fresh white breadcrumbs
1 teaspoon thyme
1 teaspoon chopped parsley
Juice of ½ lemon
2 tablespoons/30 ml oil
1 medium onion
1 oz/25 g plain flour
¾ pint/400 ml beef stock
Salt and pepper

Cut the steak into thin slices across the grain, giving pieces about 4 in./10 cm square. Mix the breadcrumbs, herbs and lemon juice and a little salt and pepper to make a crumbly stuffing which is not closely packed. Put a little stuffing on each slice and roll up, securing with cotton or a cocktail stick. Brown the beef rolls in the oil and put into the crockpot. Slice the onion thinly and cook in the oil until soft and golden. Stir in the flour and cook for 2 minutes. Add the stock and bring to the boil, stirring well. Season and pour over the meat. Cover and cook on HIGH for 30 minutes, then on LOW for 6–7 hours. Remove the cotton or cocktail sticks before serving. This dish is good with creamy mashed potatoes.

Carbonnade of Beef

1½ lb/700 g stewing steak
2 tablespoons/30 ml oil
2 large onions
2 oz/50 g lean bacon rashers
1 oz/25 g plain flour
½ pint/300 ml brown ale
Salt and pepper
1 teaspoon made mustard
½ oz/15 g sugar
1 bayleaf
Sprig of parsley
Sprig of thyme

Garnish
4 rounds French bread
1 teaspoon made mustard

Cut the steak in 2 in./5 cm cubes and brown on all sides in the oil. Add finely chopped onions and bacon and continue cooking until the onion is soft and golden. Stir in the flour and cook for 2 minutes. Add the brown ale and remaining ingredients and bring to the boil. Pour into the crockpot, cover and cook on HIGH for 30 minutes, then on LOW for 6–7 hours. Just before serving, remove the bayleaf, parsley and thyme. Toast the bread on one side only and spread mustard on the soft side. Put the bread mustard-side down on the beef just before serving.

Beef in Beer

2 lb/1 kg stewing steak
1 oz/25 g plain flour
Salt and pepper
2 tablespoons/30 ml oil
½ pint/300 ml light ale
¼ pint/150 ml beef stock
12 small onions (pickling size)
1 teaspoon vinegar
Pinch of ground mace
1 teaspoon brown sugar
1 teaspoon Worcestershire sauce

Cut the steak in 2 in./5 cm cubes and toss in flour seasoned with salt and pepper. Brown on all sides in the oil and then put the meat into the crockpot. Add the light ale, hot stock, peeled onions, vinegar, mace, sugar and Worcestershire sauce. Cover and cook on HIGH for 30 minutes, then on LOW for 6–7 hours.

Boiled Beef and Dumplings

3 lb/1·5 kg salt silverside or brisket
1 medium onion
3 medium carrots
Pepper
1 pint/500 ml water

Dumplings
4 oz/100 g self raising flour
2 oz/50 g shredded suet
Salt and pepper
4 tablespoons/60 ml water
3 lb/1·5 kg brisket or topside

Soak the beef overnight in cold water, then drain and discard the water. Slice the onion and carrots and put into the crockpot. Put the joint on top, season with pepper and pour on boiling water. Cover and cook on HIGH for 30 minutes, then on LOW for 8–10 hours. Switch to HIGH for 20 minutes before putting in the dumplings. Mix the flour, suet, seasoning and water and form into 8 balls. Put the dumplings into the crockpot and cook on HIGH for 30 minutes.

Pot-Roast Beef

3 lb/1.5 kg brisket or topside
Salt and pepper
1 oz/25 g lard
1 large onion
1 large carrot
1 pint/500 ml beef stock
1 bayleaf

Season the beef with salt and pepper and brown on all sides in the lard. Remove the beef and add the chopped onion and carrot to the fat. Cook until the onion is soft and golden. Put the vegetables into the crockpot and put the beef joint on top. Bring the stock with the bayleaf to the boil and pour over the meat. Cover and cook on HIGH for 30 minutes, then on LOW for 8–9 hours. If liked a little flour may be mixed with cold water and stirred into the crockpot an hour before serving to give a thick gravy.

Braised Brisket

2 lb/1 kg beef brisket
1 oz/25 g lard
1 lb/450 g root vegetables
1 pint/500 ml water or stock
Salt and pepper

Brown the beef brisket on all sides in the lard. Slice the vegetables thinly – a mixture of onions, carrots and potatoes can be used. Take the brisket from the fat, and cook the vegetables in the fat until just coloured. Put the vegetables in the bottom of the crockpot, and arrange the beef joint on top. Cover with boiling water or stock and season well. Cover and cook on HIGH for 30 minutes, then on LOW for 8–9 hours.

Stuffed Cabbage Rolls

12 cabbage leaves
12 oz/300 g fresh minced beef
1 small onion
1 tablespoon chopped parsley
Salt and pepper
1 oz/25 g soft brown sugar
1 lb/450 g canned tomatoes

Wash the cabbage leaves and put them into boiling water. Boil for 1 minute and drain well. Mix the minced beef, finely chopped onion, parsley and seasoning, and put a spoonful on each cabbage leaf. Fold over sides and roll into small parcels. Put into crockpot with the leaf join underneath. Sprinkle on the sugar and pour on the tomatoes with their juice. Cover and cook on HIGH for 30 minutes, then on LOW for 6–7 hours.

Veal in Cream Sauce

1½ lb/700 g stewing veal
½ oz/15 g plain flour
1 oz/25 g lard
1 small onion
3 celery sticks
Salt and pepper
1 bayleaf
Sprig of parsley
Sprig of thyme
½ pint/300 ml chicken stock
4 tablespoons/60 ml single cream

Cut the veal into 1 in./2.5 cm cubes and coat in flour. Brown on all sides in the lard. Slice the onion thinly, chop the celery and slice the carrots thinly. Put the vegetables in the crockpot with salt and pepper and herbs. Put in the veal and pour in the stock. Cover and cook on HIGH for 30 minutes, then on LOW for 8–9 hours. Just before serving, stir well and stir in the cream. Serve with rice and a green salad.

Spring Veal Casserole

1½ lb/700 g stewing veal
2 oz/50 g butter
2 tablespoons/30 ml oil
12 small onions (pickling size)
1 oz/25 g plain flour
¾ pint/400 ml chicken stock
Salt and pepper
1 lb/450 g small new potatoes
8 oz/225 shelled green peas
4 oz/100 g French beans
1 small firm lettuce heart
8 oz/225 g small new carrots
Sprig of parsley
Sprig of thyme
Sprig of marjoram

Cut the veal in 1 in./2·5 cm cubes and brown on all sides in the butter and oil. Peel the onions and put them whole into the fat, stirring well until golden. Add the flour and cook for 2 minutes, then stir in the stock and bring to the boil. Season well with salt and pepper. Scrape the potatoes and put into the casserole with the peas, beans cut in chunks, lettuce cut in quarters and scraped carrots. Pour in the veal and onions in sauce and top with the herbs. Cover and cook on HIGH for 30 minutes, then on LOW for 8–9 hours. If frozen peas and beans are used, these should be added during the last hour of cooking.

Veal Marengo

1½ lb/700 g stewing veal
1 medium onion
2 oz/50 g butter
2 tablespoons/30 ml oil
½ oz/15 g plain flour
Salt and pepper
½ pint/300 ml beef stock
2 tablespoons/30 ml tomato purée
1 bayleaf
4 oz/100 g button mushrooms

Garnish
Fried bread crumbs
1 tablespoon chopped parsley

Cut the veal in 1 in./2·5 cm cubes and chop the onion finely.
Cook in the butter and oil until the onion is soft and golden.
Stir in the flour and cook for 2 minutes. Season and add beef
stock, tomato purée, bayleaf and mushrooms cut in half. Bring
to the boil, stirring well. Pour into the crockpot, cover and cook
on HIGH for 30 minutes, then on LOW for 6–7 hours. Just
before serving, sprinkle small cubes of fried bread and the
chopped parsley on top.

Burgundy Lamb

4 oz/100 g streaky bacon rashers
1 medium onion
1 garlic clove
1½ lb/700 g shoulder lamb
1 oz/25 g plain flour
1 medium carrot
1 tablespoon/15 ml tomato purée
4 oz/100 g button mushrooms
½ pint/300 ml red wine
Salt and pepper

Chop the bacon and cook in a thick pan until the fat runs out.
Take out the bacon and fry the thinly sliced onion and chopped
garlic in the bacon fat until the onion is soft and golden. Cut
the lamb in 1 in./2·5 cm cubes and toss in the flour. Brown on
all sides in the fat. Add the thinly sliced carrot, tomato purée,
halved mushrooms, wine, salt and pepper and bring to the boil,
stirring well. Pour into the crockpot, cover and cook on HIGH
for 30 minutes, then on LOW for 6–7 hours.

Lamb and Apple Casserole

2 lb/1 kg middle neck lamb chops
1 oz/25 g plain flour
Salt and pepper
2 tablespoons/30 ml oil
2 medium onions
¾ pint/400 ml stock
2 medium carrots
1 celery stick
1 cooking apple

Coat the chops with flour seasoned with pepper and salt. Brown on both sides in the oil and remove the chops. Cook the chopped onions in the oil until soft and golden and put into the crockpot. Work any remaining flour into the fat, cook for 2 minutes, and stir in the stock. Bring to the boil, stirring well. Put the thinly sliced carrots, celery and apple into the crockpot. Put the chops on top and pour over the thickened stock, seasoning to taste. Cover and cook on HIGH for 30 minutes, then on LOW for 6–7 hours.

Irish Stew

2 lb/1 kg neck of mutton or lamb
4 medium onions
2 lb/1 kg potatoes
Salt and pepper
½ pint/300 ml stock
1 tablespoon/15 ml chopped parsley

Remove the meat from the bones and cut into small pieces.
Chop the onions finely and slice the potatoes. Put the onions,
meat and potatoes in layers in the crockpot, seasoning each
layer. Put the meat bones on top and pour over the hot stock.
Cover and cook on HIGH for 30 seconds and then on LOW for
6–7 hours. Just before serving, remove the bones and sprinkle
the stew with chopped parsley.

Spiced Lamb with Herb Dumplings

1½ lb/700 g middle neck of lamb
2 medium onions
2 medium carrots
8 oz/225 g canned tomatoes
2 tablespoons/30 ml Worcestershire sauce
1 pint/500 ml beef stock
Salt

Dumplings
4 oz/100 g self-raising flour
2 oz/50 g shredded suet
Pinch of salt
2 tablespoons chopped parsley
1 teaspoon thyme
4 tablespoons/60 ml cold water

Cut the lamb in pieces and cook in a heavy pan until browned on all sides, but do not add fat. Drain the lamb from the fat. Chop the onions finely and slice the carrots thinly. Cook the vegetables in the fat in the pan until the onions are soft and golden. Put into the crockpot and put the lamb on top. Add the tomatoes with their juice, Worcestershire sauce, stock and salt to the frying pan and bring to the boil. Pour over the lamb, cover and cook on HIGH for 30 minutes, then on LOW for 6 hours. Make the dumplings by mixing the flour, suet, salt and herbs and forming 8 balls. Switch the crockpot to HIGH for 20 minutes, add the dumplings and continue cooking on HIGH for 30 minutes.

Lamb and Tomato Casserole

2 lb/1 kg shoulder lamb
1 large onion
2 oz/50 g butter
2 tablespoons/30 ml oil
1 oz/25 g plain flour
Salt and pepper
1 teaspoon marjoram
¼ pint/150 ml beef stock
8 oz/225 g canned tomatoes

Cut the lamb into 1 in./2·5 cm cubes and chop the onions.
Cook in the butter and oil until the onions are soft and golden
and the lamb is lightly browned. Stir in the flour and cook for
2 minutes. Add seasoning, marjoram, stock and tomatoes with
their juice. Bring to the boil, stirring well. Pour into crockpot,
cover and cook on HIGH for 30 minutes, then on LOW for
6–7 hours.

Summer Lamb

8 best end neck lamb chops
1 oz/25 g lard
1 lb/450 g small new potatoes
8 oz/225 g small new carrots
Salt and pepper
Sprig of rosemary
¼ pint/150 ml water

Brown the chops on both sides in the lard. Scrape the potatoes and carrots and put into the crockpot. Season well and put the chops on top of the vegetables. Season lightly and put the rosemary on top. Pour over the water, cover and cook on HIGH for 30 minutes, then on LOW for 8–9 hours.

Arabian Lamb

8 oz/225 g mixed dried fruit
1 lemon
¾ pint/400 ml water
2 lb/1 kg shoulder lamb
1 oz/25 g plain flour
Salt and pepper
2 oz/50 g butter
2 tablespoons/30 ml oil
½ teaspoon ground ginger
½ teaspoon ground nutmeg
½ teaspoon ground cumin
½ teaspoon ground cinnamon
½ teaspoon turmeric
¼ pint/150 ml commercial soured cream

Use a mixture of dried apricots, prunes, pears, apples and peaches. Chop the fruit and remove any stones. Put into a bowl with the lemon juice and thinly peeled rind, and pour on the boiling water. Leave to stand. Cut the lamb into 2 in./5 cm cubes, coat with flour seasoned with salt and pepper, and brown on all sides in the butter and oil. Stir in the spices to coat the meat. Put the lamb into the crockpot and cover with the fruit and water used for soaking. Cover and cook on HIGH for 30 minutes, then on LOW for 6–7 hours. Just before serving, stir in the soured cream. Serve with boiled rice or noodles.

Moroccan Lamb

8 oz/225 g dried apricots
2 tablespoons/30 ml lemon juice
½ pint/300 ml water
2 oz/50 g butter
2 tablespoons/30 ml oil
1 large onion
1 garlic clove
Salt and pepper
1 teaspoon ground cinnamon
1 teaspoon ground ginger
2 lb/1 kg shoulder lamb
¾ pint/400 ml beef stock
2 oz/50 g blanched almonds
1 oz/25 g honey
1 tablespoon chopped parsley

Put the apricots into a bowl with the lemon juice and boiling water and leave to stand. Heat the butter and oil and cook the thinly sliced onion and chopped garlic until the onion is soft and golden. Stir in salt and pepper, cinnamon and ginger and then add the lamb cut in 2 in./5 cm cubes. Cook until the lamb is golden. Put into the crockpot with the drained apricots and stock. Cover and cook on HIGH for 30 minutes, then on LOW for 6–7 hours. About 30 minutes before serving time, stir in thinly sliced almonds and honey. Sprinkle chopped parsley on top just before serving.

Spiced Pork Casserole

2 lb/1 kg lean pork
½ oz/15 g curry powder
1 oz/25 g plain flour
Salt and pepper
3 medium onions
6 oz/150 g mushrooms
1 lb/450 g canned tomatoes
1 pint/500 ml chicken stock

Cut the pork into 2 in./5 cm cubes and toss in a mixture of curry powder, flour, salt and pepper. Slice the onions thinly and put on the bottom of the crockpot. Put the pork cubes on top and cover with sliced mushrooms and the tomatoes with their juice. Add the hot chicken stock, cover and cook on HIGH for 30 minutes, then on LOW for 6–7 hours.

Pork and Pepper Casserole

1½ lb/700 g lean pork
2 tablespoons/30 ml oil
1 green pepper
2 large onions
8 oz/225 g mushrooms
1 oz/25 g plain flour
½ pint/300 ml dry white wine
¼ pint/150 ml chicken stock
2 tablespoons/30 ml tomato purée
1 teaspoon sage
Salt and pepper
4 tomatoes

Cut the pork into 1 in./2·5 cm cubes and brown lightly in the oil. Add chopped pepper thinly sliced onions and sliced mushrooms and cook for 3 minutes. Stir in the flour and cook for 2 minutes. Add the wine, stock, tomato purée, sage, salt and pepper and bring to the boil. Peel the tomatoes, remove the pips and chop the flesh. Add to the hot liquid, then pour into the crockpot. Cover and cook on HIGH for 30 minutes, then on LOW for 6–7 hours.

Pork in Cider Sauce

4–6 pork chops
1 oz/25 g plain flour
Salt and pepper
2 oz/50 g lard
1 small onion
4 oz/100 g mushrooms
½ pint/300 ml dry cider

Coat the chops in flour lightly seasoned with salt and pepper, and brown on all sides in lard. Remove from the pan and drain well. Chop the onion and slice the mushrooms and cook in the lard until the onion is soft and golden. Put the onion and mushrooms in the crockpot and put the chops on top. Season with salt and pepper and pour on the cider. Cover and cook on HIGH for 30 minutes, then on LOW for 8–9 hours. A pinch of sage may be added to this dish, and a peeled sliced cooking apple may be added with the cider.

Pork in Tomato Sauce

4–6 pork chops
1 oz/25 g plain flour
Salt and pepper
2 oz/50 g lard
1 large onion
2 celery sticks
8 oz/225 g canned tomatoes
Pinch of sugar
1 teaspoon Worcestershire sauce
4 potatoes

Coat the chops with flour lightly seasoned with salt and pepper, and brown on both sides in the lard. Remove from the pan and drain well. Chop the onion finely and fry in the lard until soft and golden. Add the chopped celery, tomatoes and their juice, sugar and sauce, stir well and cook for 3 minutes. Peel the potatoes and cut in thin slices. Put into the crockpot and put the chops on top. Pour over the sauce, cover and cook on HIGH for 30 minutes, then on LOW for 8–9 hours.

Pork in Barbecue Sauce

4–6 pork chops
Salt and pepper
1 oz/25 g lard
1 medium onion
1 tablespoon/15 ml tomato purée
3 tablespoons/45 ml vinegar
1 oz/25 g soft brown sugar
1 teaspoon made mustard
2 teaspoons Worcestershire sauce
¼ pint/150 ml stock
½ oz/15 g plain flour

Season the chops with salt and pepper. Brown on both sides in
the lard, and put into the crockpot. Chop the onion finely and
cook in the fat until soft and golden. Stir in the tomato purée,
vinegar, sugar, mustard, sauce and stock and bring to the boil.
Pour over the chops, cover and cook on HIGH for 30 minutes,
then on LOW for 6–7 hours. About 30 minutes before serving,
mix the flour with a little cold water and stir into the sauce,
and continue cooking.

Pork with Red Cabbage

2 lb/1 kg lean pork
2 oz/50 g butter
2 tablespoons/30 ml oil
1 medium red cabbage
1 cooking apple
½ pint/300 ml red wine
2 teaspoons soft brown sugar
Salt and pepper

Cut the pork into 2 in./5 cm cubes and cook in butter and oil until golden on all sides. Put into the crockpot. Remove tough outer leaves from the cabbage, and shred the rest finely. Put into boiling water, boil for 5 minutes and drain well. Put on top of the pork with the peeled and chopped apple, wine, sugar, salt and pepper. Cover and cook on HIGH for 30 minutes, then on LOW for 7–8 hours. Stir well before serving. This dish is good with plainly boiled or baked jacket potatoes.

Pork and Apple Bake

1 lb/450 g potatoes
8 oz/225 g onions
4 pork chops
2 pig's kidneys
2 oz/50 g lard
1 cooking apple
2 teaspoons sage
Salt and pepper
1 tablespoon/15 ml tomato sauce
½ pint/300 ml water

Peel the potatoes and onion and cut them in very thin slices. Wipe the chops and skin and slice the kidneys. Brown the chops and kidneys on all sides in the lard. Put the potatoes and onions in the bottom of the crockpot. Top with the chops and kidneys. Add the peeled sliced apple, sage, salt and pepper. Boil the water, stir in the tomato sauce and pour over the chops. Cover and cook on HIGH for 30 minutes, then on LOW for 8–9 hours.

Pork in Orange Sauce

4–6 pork chops
Salt and pepper
2 oz/50 g butter
2 tablespoons/30 ml oil
½ pint/300 ml orange juice
2 tablespoons/30 ml bottled sauce
1 teaspoon grated orange rind
1 teaspoon soft brown sugar
Pinch of ground ginger
1 orange

Season the chops with salt and pepper and brown on both sides in the butter and oil. Put into the crockpot and add the orange juice, sauce, orange rind, sugar and ginger. Cover and cook on HIGH for 30 minutes, then on LOW for 6–7 hours. Just before serving, peel the orange and cut in slices, and put on top of the chops.

Sausage Pot

4 oz/100 g slice of bacon
8 oz/225 g onions
1 lb/450 g large pork sausages
12 oz/300 g potatoes
Pepper
½ pint/300 ml water
1 teaspoon chopped parsley

Cut the slice of bacon into small cubes and put into a heavy pan. Cook gently until the fat runs. Slice the onions thinly and cook with the bacon until the onions are soft and golden. Put into the crockpot. Brown the sausages in the fat and arrange on top of the bacon and onion. Peel the potatoes and cut in thin slices. Add to the crockpot with the pepper and pour over boiling water. Cover and cook on HIGH for 30 minutes, then on LOW for 7–8 hours. Sprinkle parsley on top before serving.

Boiled Bacon

2 lb/1 kg bacon joint
½ oz/15 g soft brown sugar
1 bayleaf

Soak the joint overnight and discard the water. Put into the crockpot with the sugar and bayleaf and cover with fresh boiling water. Cook on HIGH for 30 minutes, then on LOW for 6–7 hours. Remove from the cooking liquid and strip off the skin before serving. The bacon stock is good for making pea or lentil soup.

Apple Bacon

3 lb/1.5 kg collar bacon joint
1 pint/500 ml apple juice
4 cloves
6 peppercorns
2 small onions (pickling size)
½ oz/15 g soft brown sugar

Soak the bacon in cold water overnight (this is not necessary if the bacon is Danish). Drain the bacon and put into fresh cold water. Bring to the boil slowly, then drain the bacon joint and put into the crockpot. Put the apple juice, cloves, peppercorns, peeled whole onions and sugar into a saucepan and bring to the boil. Pour over the bacon and add a little hot water if necessary so that the bacon is just covered. Cover and cook on HIGH for 30 minutes, then on LOW for 6–7 hours. Take bacon from crockpot, remove skin and slice to serve with a little of the cooking liquid as gravy. Try this with fried potatoes and a green vegetable.

Bacon Hotpot

3 lb/1.5 kg collar bacon joint
2 oz/50 g lard
12 small onions (pickling size)
12 small carrots
4 leeks
¾ pint/400 ml water
Pepper
1 bayleaf
Sprig of parsley
Sprig of thyme

Soak the bacon overnight (this will not be necessary if the bacon is Danish). Drain well and cut the bacon into 1 in./2.5 cm cubes. Put into a pan with cold water, bring slowly to the boil and then drain. Heat the lard and cook the bacon, peeled whole onions, whole carrots and chopped leeks until the onions are soft and golden. Put into the crockpot, pour over boiling water and add the pepper and herbs. Cover and cook on HIGH for 30 minutes, then on LOW for 7–8 hours. Remove herbs before serving.

Bacon and Beans

1 lb/450 g butter beans
2 lb/1 kg unsmoked bacon joint
1 oz/25 g butter
2 tablespoons/30 ml oil
1 large onion
4 celery sticks
2 large carrots
1 pint/500 ml water
Pepper
1 tablespoon chopped parsley

Put the beans into cold water and bring to the boil. Boil for 5
minutes, remove from heat, cover and leave to stand for 1 hour.
Remove the rind and excess fat from the bacon and cut the
bacon into 1 in./2·5 cm cubes. Put into a pan with cold water,
bring slowly to the boil and then drain. Heat the butter and oil
in a thick pan and cook the bacon, chopped onion, celery and
finely sliced carrots until the onion is soft and golden. Add the
water and bring to the boil. Season with pepper and pour into
the crockpot. Add the drained beans and stir well. Cover and
cook on HIGH for 30 minutes, then on LOW for 8 hours.
Serve sprinkled with chopped parsley.

Bacon in Cider Sauce

2 lb/1 kg bacon joint
8 cloves
1 small onion
1 eating apple
2 lb/1 kg small new potatoes
½ pint/300 ml dry cider
Sprig of rosemary
Pepper

Soak the bacon in cold water overnight (this will not be necessary if the bacon is Danish). Drain and remove the skin. Stick the cloves into the bacon fat and put the joint into the crockpot. Surround with the finely chopped onion and apple and with the scraped potatoes. Bring the cider to the boil and pour over the bacon. Add the rosemary and season with pepper. Cover and cook on HIGH for 30 minutes, then on LOW for 8–9 hours. Serve the bacon in thick slices with the potatoes. Remove the rosemary and boil the cooking liquid with onion and apple in a separate pan until thick to use as sauce with the bacon.

Bacon in Beer

2 lb/1 kg collar bacon joint
1 medium onion
1 medium carrot
Pepper
1 tablespoon/15 ml black treacle
¾ pint/400 ml brown ale
1 bayleaf
1 oz/25 g butter
1 oz/25 g plain flour

Soak the bacon overnight (this will not be necessary if the bacon is Danish). Drain and remove the skin. Put into the crockpot with finely chopped onion and carrot. Season with pepper and treacle, pour over the ale and add the bayleaf. Cover and cook on HIGH for 30 minutes, then on LOW for 8–9 hours. About 30 minutes before serving, work the butter and flour together and stir into the crockpot. Continue heating until serving time.

Liver and Bacon Casserole

1 lb/450 g lamb's or pig's liver
1 oz/25 g plain flour
Salt and pepper
6 streaky bacon rashers
1 small onion
¼ pint/150 ml beef stock

Wash and dry the liver and cut in thin slices. Coat in flour seasoned with salt and pepper. Cook in the lard until just coloured. Fry the bacon rashers lightly in the same fat, and the chopped onion until soft and golden. Put the bacon and onion in the crockpot and top with the liver slices. Work any remaining flour into the fat, cook for 2 minutes and add the stock. Bring to the boil, stirring well, and pour over the liver. Cover and cook on HIGH for 30 minutes, then on LOW for 6–7 hours.

Spanish Liver

1 lb/450 g pig's or lamb's liver
4 streaky bacon rashers
2 medium carrots
2 celery sticks
1 small onion
1 lb/450 g canned tomatoes
Salt and pepper
1 bayleaf

Cut the liver in thin slices. Chop the bacon and put into a thick pan. Heat gently until the fat runs and then brown the liver lightly on each side. Take out the bacon and liver. Chop the carrots, celery and onion finely and cook in the bacon fat until the onion is soft and golden. Put into the crockpot with the liver and bacon on top. Pour on the tomatoes with their juice and season with salt and pepper. Add the bayleaf. Cover and cook on HIGH for 30 minutes, then on LOW for 6–7 hours.

Liver and Potato Casserole

1 lb/450 g lamb's or pig's liver
2 large onions
2 oz/50 g lard
½ oz/15 g plain flour
Salt and pepper
½ pint/300 ml beef stock
1 lb/450 g potatoes
1 teaspoon sage
6 streaky bacon rashers

Cut the liver in thin slices. Slice the onions thinly. Brown the liver on all sides in the lard and put on one side. Cook the onions in the lard until soft and golden. Stir in the flour and cook for 2 minutes. Add the seasoning and stock and stir until boiling. Peel the potatoes and slice them thinly. Put into the crockpot and cover with the onions. Put the liver on top and add the sage leaves and bacon rashers. Cover and cook on HIGH for 30 minutes, then on LOW for 8–9 hours.

Faggots

1 lb/450 g pig's liver
2 large onions
6 oz/150 g fresh white breadcrumbs
2 oz/50 g shredded suet
Pinch of sage
1 tablespoon/15 ml Worcestershire sauce
Salt and pepper
1 oz/25 g lard
1 medium onion
2 medium carrots
1 oz/25 g plain flour
¾ pint/400 ml beef stock

Mince the liver and onions and mix with the breadcrumbs, suet, sage, sauce and seasoning. Divide into 8 pieces and form into balls. Melt the lard and brown the liver balls on all sides. Drain and put into the crockpot. Slice the onion thinly and cook in the lard until soft and golden. Add grated carrot and flour and stir well. Cook for 2 minutes then stir in the stock. Bring to the boil, stirring well, then pour over the liver balls. Cover and cook on HIGH for 30 minutes, then on LOW for 6–7 hours. Serve with creamy mashed potatoes.

Kidney Stew

10 lamb's kidneys
1 small onion
1 oz/25 g lard
2 oz/50 g mushrooms
2 tablespoons/30 ml tomato purée
¼ pint/150 ml beef stock
Salt and pepper
1 tablespoon chopped parsley

Skin the kidneys, remove the cores and cut the kidneys in half lengthwise. Chop the onion finely. Cook the kidneys and onion in the lard until the kidneys are just coloured. Put into the crockpot with sliced mushrooms, tomato purée, stock, salt and pepper. Cover and cook on HIGH for 30 minutes, then on LOW for 6–7 hours. Sprinkle with parsley just before serving.

Stuffed Hearts

6 lambs' hearts
2 oz/50 g plain flour
2 medium onions
2 medium carrots
2 celery sticks
1 pint/500 ml beef stock
Salt and pepper

Stuffing
1 medium onion
3 oz/75 g fresh white breadcrumbs
2 tablespoons/30 ml chopped parsley
Pinch of thyme
1 egg
Salt and pepper

Slit the top of each heart lengthwise, remove blood vessels and hollow out room for the stuffing. Leave the hearts to soak in cold water for 1 hour. Make the stuffing by mixing the finely chopped onion, breadcrumbs, herbs, egg and seasoning and fill each heart. Fix the tops with cocktail sticks and roll the hearts in flour. Put into the crockpot and arrange thinly sliced onions, carrots and celery round them. Heat the stock and pour over the hearts, seasoning well. Cover and cook on HIGH for 30 minutes, then on LOW for 8–10 hours.

Oxtail Casserole

1 oxtail
1 oz/25 g plain flour
Salt and pepper
2 oz/50 g lard
2 large onions
4 medium carrots
2 medium turnips
1 pint/500 ml beef stock

Cut the oxtail in pieces and toss in flour seasoned with salt and pepper. Heat the lard and brown the pieces of oxtail on all sides. Put on one side. Slice the onions thinly and cook in the fat until golden. Slice the carrots thinly and chop the turnips. Arrange the onions, carrots and turnips in the crockpot and put the oxtail pieces on top. Add the hot stock and some additional seasoning. Cover and cook on HIGH for 30 minutes, then on LOW for 8–10 hours.

Tongue

1 ox tongue
1 medium onion
8 peppercorns
Pinch of salt
1 bayleaf
2 pints/1 l water

Soak the tongue in cold water overnight. Drain the tongue and put into the crockpot, curling into shape. Add the chopped onion, peppercorns, salt, bayleaf and hot water. Cover and cook on HIGH for 1 hour, then on LOW for 12–14 hours. Drain the tongue and take off skin and gristle, and remove any small bones at the root of the tongue. Put into a round cake tin or straight-sided bowl (such as a soufflé dish), curling the tongue into a neat shape. Cover with a plate or saucer and put on a heavy weight. Leave until cold and set before turning out. Hot tongue is also delicious if left uncurled, cut in thick slices and served with mushroom sauce or a rich brown gravy flavoured with redcurrant jelly or cranberry sauce.

Tripe and Mushrooms

1 lb/450 g tripe
2 tablespoons/30 ml vinegar
2 tablespoons/30 ml olive oil
2 oz/50 g butter
2 tablespoons/30 ml oil
1 small onion
8 oz/225 g mushrooms
1 oz/25 g plain flour
1 lb/450 g canned tomatoes
Salt and pepper
4 oz/100 g fresh white breadcrumbs

Cut the tripe into strips 1 in./2·5 cm wide and 2 in./5 cm long and leave in vinegar and olive oil for 30 minutes. Heat the butter and oil and cook the finely chopped onion and sliced mushrooms until the onion is soft and golden. Work in the flour and cook for 2 minutes. Add the tomatoes and their juice and bring to the boil, stirring well. Season with salt and pepper. Put a layer of tripe in the crockpot. Pour on half the tomato mixture and top with half the breadcrumbs. Put on remaining tripe, then tomato mixture and crumbs. Cover and cook on HIGH for 30 minutes, then on LOW for 6–7 hours.

Tripe Rolls in Cider

1 lb/450 g tripe
8 streaky bacon rashers
Salt and pepper
Pinch of ground nutmeg
1 teaspoon mixed herbs
3 medium carrots
3 medium onions
¾ pint/400 ml dry cider

Cut the tripe into narrow slices and put a bacon rasher on each one. Sprinkle with salt and pepper, nutmeg and herbs and roll up securely, tying with cotton. Slice the carrots and onions very thinly and put into the crockpot. Top with the tripe rolls. Bring the cider just to the boil and pour into the crockpot. Cover and cook on HIGH for 30 minutes, then on LOW for 8–9 hours.

Normandy Tripe

2 lb/1 kg tripe
1 cowheel
2 medium carrots
2 medium onions
2 leeks
2 streaky bacon rashers
3 cloves
1 bayleaf
Sprig of parsley
Sprig of thyme
Salt and pepper
Pinch of cayenne pepper
1 pint/500 ml dry cider
4 tablespoons/60 ml Calvados or brandy

Cut the tripe into small pieces. Split the cowheel (if your butcher cannot supply a cowheel, he should have a pig's trotter to use instead). Slice the carrots thinly chop the onions and slice the leeks thinly. Chop the bacon in small pieces. Put the vegetables and bacon into the crockpot. Put in the cowheel, cloves, tripe, herbs and seasoning. Bring the cider to the boil and pour into the crockpot with the Calvados or brandy. Cover and cook on HIGH for 30 minutes, then on LOW for 10–12 hours. Remove the cowheel, cloves and herbs and stir well before serving.

Vegetables and Pulses

Complete vegetable meals are becoming very popular. A dish of mixed vegetables can be delicious on its own with bread and butter. For a more substantial vegetarian meal, poached eggs or some grated cheese may be added at the last minute. Others may like to add grilled bacon, a slice of cold cooked meat, grilled or fried fish, roast or grilled meat or poultry. A vegetable dish may be prepared in the crockpot for all-day cooking, leaving only quick and easy cooking of the protein accompaniment to complete a meal.

Root vegetables take a long time to prepare in the crockpot, but vegetables which contain a lot of liquid such as marrows, courgettes and tomatoes cook more quickly. They can be usefully combined with the root vegetables to give liquid which is full of flavour in which the harder vegetables cook gently. Canned tomatoes are particularly useful to give flavour and colour to one-pot vegetable dishes. Little liquid should be added to vegetables cooked in the crockpot as steam is created by this method of cooking and the liquid does not evaporate. Chicken or beef stock can be used instead of water, and a little dry white wine or cider goes well with many vegetables. A little butter or oil gives flavour to vegetable dishes.

Cut all vegetables in small pieces, either slicing, chopping or dicing, and place hard root vegetables in the bottom of the crockpot, topping with softer vegetables and liquid. Frozen vegetables may be added to dishes, but should be partly thawed before adding to the crockpot so that they do not reduce the working temperature too far. They usually need only $\frac{1}{2}$–1 hour in the crockpot. Leafy green vegetables are not really suited to crockpot cooking, although red cabbage is delicious prepared as a casserole. Dried vegetables can be used in a crockpot to give additional flavouring (e.g. onions, peppers or mixed vegetables) but it is wise to read the label on the jar to see if they should be soaked in water before use.

Pulses such as dried beans, peas and lentils are normally soaked overnight before cooking. This is not entirely satisfactory for the crockpot, and I prefer to part-cook them, then leave them to stand in the cooking liquid for an hour before use (individual times are given in recipes). Many different types of pulses are now available and are worth experimenting with in the crockpot. I have specified haricot beans for most of the recipes as these are easily obtainable, but other types may be substituted when you find them. If you find the initial preparation of beans tiresome, drained canned beans (such as kidney beans) can be used but are usually rather expensive.

Braised Carrots and Courgettes

1 lb/500 g carrots
3 medium courgettes
1 medium onion
¼ pint/150 ml chicken stock
Salt and pepper
Pinch of tarragon
1 oz/25 g butter

Peel the carrots and slice them thinly. Wash the courgettes but do not peel them. Slice them thinly and mix with the carrots and the finely chopped onion. Put into the crockpot and add the stock with seasoning and tarragon. Stir well and put flakes of butter on top. Cover and cook on LOW for 6–7 hours.

Braised Celery

4 oz/100 g butter
8 celery hearts
1 pint/500 ml chicken or beef stock
Salt and pepper

Soften the butter slightly and rub it around the inside of the crockpot. Wash the celery hearts very thoroughly and trim them. Put into the crockpot and pour on hot stock. Season well. Cover and cook on HIGH for 3 hours. Braised celery is particularly good with beef, and the cooking liquid makes an excellent base for soup.

Braised Leeks

10 leeks
¼ pint/150 ml chicken stock
4 tablespoons/60 ml dry white wine
Salt and pepper
1 oz/25 g butter

Trim the roots and green tops from the leeks so that they fit neatly into the crockpot in two layers. Mix the stock and wine with seasoning and pour over the leeks. Put flakes of butter on top. Cover and cook on LOW for 4–5 hours.

Aubergine Casserole

1 large aubergine
2 large onions
1 oz/25 g plain flour
3 tablespoons/45 ml olive oil
Salt and pepper
¼ pint/150 ml beef stock

Peel the aubergine and onions. Cut the aubergine in 1 in./2·5 cm slices and coat in the flour. Heat the oil and brown the aubergine slices. Add the thinly sliced onions and cook them until golden. Put the aubergine and onions in the crockpot, seasoning well. Pour on the stock and put flakes of butter on top. Cover and cook on LOW for 5–6 hours. If your crockpot has a stoneware liner which can be lifted out for service, the top of the vegetables can be covered with a layer of breadcrumbs and dotted with butter, and the top browned under the grill before serving.

Summer Vegetable Casserole

1 oz/25 g butter
3 streaky bacon rashers
1 medium onion
1 garlic clove
2 tablespoons/30 ml olive oil
2 medium carrots
2 tomatoes
4 oz/100 g button mushrooms
Salt and pepper
Pinch of nutmeg
1 bayleaf
¼ pint/150 ml chicken stock
8 oz/225 g shelled peas

Chop the bacon and heat in a thick pan until the fat begins to run. Add the finely chopped onion and crushed garlic, with the olive oil, and cook until soft and golden. Put into the crockpot. Peel the carrots and cut them into small dice. Peel the tomatoes, remove the seeds and chop the flesh. Wipe the mushrooms and leave them whole. Put the vegetables into the crockpot with the seasoning, bayleaf and stock. Cover and cook on LOW for 5–6 hours. Put the peas into the crockpot 2 hours before the end of cooking time. Serve alone with crusty bread, or use as an accompaniment to meat, poultry, or fish.

Buttered Potatoes

8 medium potatoes
1 tablespoon/15 ml chopped parsley
Pinch of thyme
Pinch of tarragon
1 tablespoon/15 ml chopped chives
Salt and pepper
4 oz/100 g butter

Peel the potatoes and slice them very thinly. Put them in the crockpot and sprinkle with the herbs and seasoning. Melt the butter and pour over the potatoes. Mix well, cover and cook on LOW for 6–7 hours.

Mediterranean Beans

1 lb/500 g French beans
8 oz/300 g canned tomatoes
1 medium onion
1 garlic clove
Pinch of marjoram
1 teaspoon/5 ml lemon juice
1 tablespoon/15 ml olive oil
Salt and pepper

Use very young beans and cut them into 1 in./2·5 cm lengths.
Put into the crockpot and cover with the tomatoes and juice
from the can. Break up the tomatoes with a fork and sprinkle
on the very finely chopped onion and crushed garlic cloves. Put
in the marjoram, lemon juice, oil and seasoning and stir well.
Cover and cook on LOW for 5–6 hours.

Carrots in Wine Sauce

1 lb/500 g carrots
3 shallots
Pinch of thyme
Pinch of tarragon
Salt and pepper
¼ pint/150 ml dry white wine
1 teaspoon/5 ml lemon juice
1 oz/25 g butter

Peel the carrots and slice them very thinly. Put them in the crockpot and cover with finely chopped shallots. Sprinkle with the herbs and seasoning, and pour in the wine and lemon juice. Top with flakes of butter. Cover and cook on LOW for 6–7 hours.

Cauliflower in Tomato Sauce

2 tablespoons/30 ml oil
1 onion
1 garlic clove
1 lb/500 g canned tomatoes
¼ pint/150 ml water
1 cauliflower
8 black olives
½ teaspoon/2.5 ml basil
Salt and pepper

Chop onions and cook in oil until soft. Drain and put into crockpot with crushed garlic, tomatoes and water. Add the cauliflower in pieces. Cook on HIGH for 30 minutes, then on LOW for 3 hours. Just before serving, add chives, basil and seasoning to taste.

Red Cabbage Casserole

1 oz/25 g butter
1 small onion
1 small red cabbage
1 cooking apple
2 tablespoons/30 ml wine vinegar
2 tablespoons/30 ml water
½ oz/15 g soft brown sugar
1 tablespoon/15 ml red currant jelly
Salt and pepper
1 teaspoon/5 ml ground mixed spice

Heat the butter and cook the finely chopped onion until soft and golden. Add the finely shredded cabbage. Peel, core and slice the apple and add to the vegetales. Add the remaining ingredients and stir until hot. Put into the crockpot and cook on LOW for 8–9 hours. This is a delicious way of cooking red cabbage which is particularly good served with fat meats such as pork, goose or duck.

Potato and Tomato Bake

1 tablespoon/15 ml oil
2 large onions
1 lb 12 oz/800 g canned tomatoes
2 teaspoons/10 ml marjoram
2 lb/1 kg potatoes
Salt and pepper
½ oz/15 g plain flour
2 oz/50 g grated Cheddar cheese

Heat the oil and cook the finely chopped onions for 3 minutes until soft and golden. Strain the liquid from the tomatoes and keep it in reserve. Mix the marjoram with the tomatoes. Peel the potatoes and cut them in thin slices. Put half the potatoes in the crockpot, then half the tomatoes and half the onions, seasoning each layer well. Top with a second layer of potatoes, tomatoes and onions. Stir the flour into any oil which remains in the cooking pan and cook for 1 minute. Stir in the reserved tomato juice and bring to the boil. Season well and pour over the vegetables. Cook on HIGH for 15 minutes and then on LOW for 8 hours. Sprinkle with grated cheese just before serving.

Courgettes with Tomatoes

2 lb/1 kg courgettes
1 small green pepper
1 small onion
1 garlic clove
Salt and pepper
8 oz/225 g tomatoes
2 oz/50 g butter
1 tablespoon/15 ml chopped parsley

Wipe the courgettes but do not peel them. Cut them in thin slices and put them into the crockpot. Chop the pepper and onion finely and crush the garlic. Mix well together and put on top of the courgettes. Sprinkle well with salt and pepper. Peel the tomatoes and cut them in thin slices. Arrange the slices on top of the other vegetables and dot with flakes of butter. Cover and cook on HIGH for 3 hours. Sprinkle with parsley and serve as an accompaniment to meat, poultry or fish.

Ratatouille

2 large onions
2 green peppers
1 lb/500 g tomatoes
1 aubergine
4 courgettes
1 garlic clove
4 tablespoons/60 ml oil
Salt and pepper

Peel the onions and cut them in thin slices. Remove the stems, seeds and membranes from the peppers and cut the flesh in thin slices. Skin the tomatoes and cut them in half. Take out the seeds and cut the flesh into pieces. Wipe the aubergine and courgettes but do not peel them before cutting into thin slices. Put all the vegetables into the crockpot with the crushed garlic, oil and seasoning and stir well together. Cook on HIGH for 30 minutes, and then on LOW for 8 hours. Season again before serving if necessary. Serve hot or cold as a single dish, or as an accompaniment to meat, poultry, or fish.

Vegetable Rice

12 oz/350 g long grain rice
¼ pint/150 ml olive oil
½ pint/300 ml tomato juice
½ pint/300 ml water
4 oz/100 g mushrooms
1 medium onion
1 green pepper
Salt and pepper

Heat the oil and cook the rice gently, stirring well, until the rice is golden brown. Drain off surplus oil, and put the rice into the crockpot. Add the tomato juice and water. Slice the mushrooms and onion very finely, and chop the pepper finely. Stir into the crockpot together with the seasoning. Cover and cook on LOW for 6 hours, stirring once, an hour before serving. A little chopped bacon is a good addition to this dish, or some small pieces of smoked haddock.

Stuffed Green Peppers

6 small green peppers
4 oz/100 g cooked long grain rice
4 oz/100 g cooked ham or bacon
2 oz/50 g mushrooms
1 small onion
2 tablespoons/30 ml tomato sauce
Salt and pepper
¼ pint/150 ml beef or chicken stock
1 oz/25 g butter

Cut the peppers in half from stem to base and take out the
membranes and seeds. Mix together the rice, finely chopped
ham or bacon, mushrooms and onions and moisten with the
tomato sauce. Season well and fill the pepper halves. Arrange
them in the cockpot and pour in the stock. Put a small flake of
butter on each pepper half, cover and cook on LOW for 6–7
hours. If preferred, 4 large peppers may be used.

Baked Onions

6 medium onions
4 oz/100 g grated Cheddar cheese
2 oz/50 g fresh white breadcrumbs
Salt and pepper
¼ pint/150 ml beef stock

Peel the onions, put them into boiling water and boil for 2 minutes. Drain thoroughly and cool the onions slightly. Remove the cores of the onions with an apple corer. Mix the cheese, breadcrumbs and seasoning and fill the centres of the onions with the mixture, pressing it down firmly. Put the filled onions into the crockpot and pour on the hot stock. Cover and cook on LOW for 6–7 hours.

Stuffed Marrow

1 small marrow
8 oz/225 g cooked meat
1 small onion
½ pint/300 ml thick gravy
1 teaspoon/5 ml Worcestershire sauce
Salt and pepper

Peel the marrow and cut it in half, scooping out the seeds and fibres. Mince the meat and onion and mix with the gravy, Worcestershire sauce, salt and pepper. Fill the marrow halves with the meat mixture. Wrap each half in foil, keeping the closing at the top. Put into the crockpot and pour in ¼ pint/150 ml hot water. Cook on LOW for 8–9 hours. Lift out of the foil and serve with vegetables and additional gravy.

Bean Hotpot

8 oz/225 g haricot beans
1 pint/500 ml water
1 medium onion
2 teaspoons/10 ml mustard powder
Salt and pepper
1 oz/25 g black treacle

Wash the beans, cover them with the water with a pinch of
salt, and bring to the boil. Simmer for 10 minutes, remove
from the heat, cover and leave to stand for 1 hour. Cut the
onion into thin slices and put into the crockpot. Sprinkle with
mustard and put in the beans and liquid. Season well and stir
in the treacle. Cover and cook on LOW for 8–9 hours. Serve as
a complete meal with crusty or brown bread, or add some
slices of crisply cooked bacon or grilled pork chops or slices.

Boston Baked Beans

1 lb/500 g haricot beans
2 pints/1 l water
4 oz/100 g salt pork
1 medium onion
3 oz/75 g soft brown sugar
2 oz/50 g black treacle
1 teaspoon/5 ml mustard powder
1 teaspoon/5 ml salt
Pepper

Put the beans into the water and bring to the boil. Simmer for 10 minutes, then remove from the heat, cover and leave to stand for 1 hour. Put into the crockpot with the cooking liquid. Chop the pork and onions in small pieces, and add to the crockpot with the other ingredients. Stir well, cover and cook on LOW for 10–12 hours. A little concentrated tomato purée (about 1 tablespoon/15 ml) may be stirred into the beans if liked. Try serving these beans as a complete meal with plenty of brown bread.

Savoury Beans

1 lb/500 g haricot or flageolet beans
1 pint/500 ml water
½ pint/300 ml chicken stock
1 medium onion
1 bayleaf
Pinch of thyme
Pinch of rosemary
Salt and pepper

When this dish is made with flageolet beans, it is a perfect accompaniment to roast lamb. 'Flageolets' are the small green beans from the French bean which are dried, but harricot beans may be used instead if these are unobtainable. Put the beans into the water and bring to the boil. Simmer for 10 minutes, take off the heat, cover and leave to stand for 1 hour. Put the beans and cooking liquid into the crockpot with the chicken stock, finely chopped onion, herbs and seasoning. Cover and cook on LOW for 8–9 hours.

Crockpot Cassoulet

1 lb/500 g haricot beans
1 lb/500 g shoulder lamb
2 tablespoons/30 ml oil
8 oz/225 g smoked gammon
1 medium onion
2 garlic cloves
2 oz/50 g concentrated tomato purée
Pinch of thyme
1 teaspoon/5 ml salt
Pepper
¼ pint/150 ml dry white wine
2 pints/1 l water

Put the beans into a pan with half the water. Bring to the boil and simmer for 10 minutes. Remove from the heat, cover and leave to stand for 1 hour. Cut the lamb into 1 in./2·5 cm cubes and cook in the oil until brown. Grill the piece of gammon and then cut into 1 in./2·5 cm pieces. Chop the onion finely and crush the garlic cloves. Put the beans and cooking liquid into the crockpot with the lamb, gammon, onion and garlic. Add the tomato purée, thyme, salt and pepper, wine and remaining water. Stir well, cover and cook on LOW for 10–12 hours.

Lentils and Sausages

1 lb/500 g lentils
¾ pint/400 ml water
1 medium onion
1 garlic clove
1 bayleaf
¾ pint/400 ml beef stock
1 lb/500 g smoked sausage

Put the lentils into the water and bring to the boil. Simmer for
10 minutes, remove from the heat, cover and leave to stand for
1 hour. Put the lentils and cooking liquid into the crockpot with
the finely chopped onion, crushed garlic, bayleaf and beef
stock. Cut the sausage into 2 in./5 cm lengths. Stir into the
lentils, cover and cook on LOW for 8–9 hours. Smoked sausage
rings are available in delicatessen shops and many grocers.

Sauces and Dips

Some sauces which require long slow cooking, such as meat sauce for spaghetti, are ideal for crockpot cooking. All-day or overnight cooking will blend the flavours and give a rich smooth texture. When cooking is completed, the sauces may be served with plainly cooked meat, poultry or fish, or with rice or pasta. It is worth preparing some of these sauces for freezing, and if your crockpot is large enough, double the recipes and serve what is needed for a meal, freezing the rest in convenient portions.

Hot dips, such as fondues, can also be prepared in the crockpot and kept hot on the LOW setting, so that the crockpot may be used as a container into which pieces of food may be dipped.

Curry Sauce

1 oz/25 g lard
1 medium onion
1 tablespoon/15 ml curry powder
½ oz/15 g plain flour
½ pint/300 ml beef stock
1 tablespoon/15 ml tomato purée
1 tablespoon/15 ml chutney
2 teaspoons/10 ml lemon juice
2 oz/50 g sultanas
Pinch of salt

Melt the lard in a thick pan and fry the finely chopped onion until golden and soft. Stir in the curry powder and flour and cook for 3 minutes. Take off the heat and stir in the stock, tomato purée, chutney, lemon juice, sultanas and salt. Stir well to blend ingredients and put into crockpot. Cook on LOW for 4–5 hours. This sauce may be used over hard-boiled eggs or grilled meat or poultry. Cold cooked meat, poultry or fish may be added to the sauce for the last hour of cooking, and the crockpot should be set to HIGH for the last hour.

Tomato Sauce

1½ lb/700 g tomatoes
1 oz/25 g butter
1 small onion
2 medium carrots
2 celery sticks
2 oz/50 g bacon
1 bayleaf
6 peppercorns
1 sprig of parsley
1 pint/500 ml water
Salt and pepper
1 oz/25 g plain flour

Dip the tomatoes in boiling water and remove their skins. Cut the tomatoes in quarters and put into the crockpot. Melt the butter in a heavy pan and fry the chopped onion, sliced carrots, chopped celery and bacon until the onion is soft and golden. Put into the tomatoes with the bayleaf, peppercorns, parsley, water, salt and pepper. Cover and cook on LOW for 8–9 hours. Sieve the sauce. Mix the flour with a spoonful of water and stir into the sauce. Return to the crockpot and heat on LOW for 30 minutes.

Meat Sauce for Spaghetti

1 oz/25 g lard
1 lb/450 g fresh minced beef
1 medium onion
2 oz/50 g mushrooms
1 lb/450 canned tomatoes
1 bayleaf
Salt and pepper
Pinch of mixed herbs

Melt the lard and cook the minced beef and finely chopped
onion for 5 minutes, stirring well. Put into the crockpot with
finely chopped mushrooms, tomatoes and liquid from the can,
bayleaf, seasoning and herbs. Cover and cook on LOW for 6–7
hours. A little red wine may be substituted for some of the
liquid from the canned tomatoes.

Espagnole Sauce

2 oz/50 g lean bacon
2 oz/50 g butter
1 small onion
1 medium carrot
2 oz/50 g mushrooms
1 oz/25 g plain flour
2 tablespoons/30 ml tomato purée
1 pint/500 ml bone stock
Salt and pepper
2 tablespoons/30 ml sherry

Chop the bacon finely and put into a heavy pan. Heat gently until the fat begins to run. Add the butter and finely chopped onion, carrot and mushrooms. Cook until the onion is soft and golden. Lift out of the pan with a slotted spoon and put into the crockpot. Stir the flour into the juices left in the pan and cook until lightly browned. Take off the heat and stir in the tomato purée, stock and seasoning. When well blended, pour over the vegetables in the crockpot. Cook on LOW for 6–7 hours. Strain the sauce and stir in the sherry just before using.

Sweet and Sour Sauce

2 medium onions
2 celery sticks
2 carrots
2 oz/50 g soft brown sugar
2 teaspoons/10 ml made mustard
3 tablespoons/45 ml tomato purée
1 pint/500 ml pineapple juice
Juice of 1 lemon
Salt and pepper

Chop the onions and celery finely, and slice the carrots thinly and put into the crockpot with the other ingredients, cover and cook on HIGH for 3–4 hours. If liked, some chopped pineapple chunks may be added to the sauce before cooking. This sauce may be used with grilled meat, poultry or fish. If preferred, lean pork, lamb or chicken may be cut into 1 in./2·5 cm cubes and sealed in hot oil before being put into the crockpot at the beginning of cooking.

Barbecue Sauce

1 small onion
½ pint/300 ml bottled sauce
1 tablespoon/15 ml Worcestershire sauce
2 drops Tabasco sauce
½ pint/300 ml water
3 tablespoons/45 ml vinegar
½ oz/15 g soft brown sugar
½ oz/15 g salt

Chop the onion very finely and put into the crockpot with the other ingredients. Stir well, cover and cook on LOW for 3 hours. Use with steak, chops, chicken, spareribs or sausages.

Rich Mushroom Sauce

½ oz/15 g butter
1 small onion
6 oz/150 g mushrooms
¼ pint/150 ml red wine
¼ pint/150 ml beef stock
½ oz/15 g cornflour
1 tablespoon/15 ml Worcestershire sauce
Salt and pepper

Melt the butter and fry the finely chopped onion for 3 minutes.
Add the chopped mushrooms and fry for 2 minutes. Put into
the crockpot with the wine and stock. Cover and cook on LOW
for 3–4 hours. Thirty minutes before serving, mix the cornflour,
Worcestershire sauce, seasoning and a little of the hot sauce.
Blend well and return to crockpot, cover and continue cooking
for 30 minutes. Serve with grilled steak or chops, with chicken
or fish, or with roast beef.

Cranberry Sauce

2 lb/1 kg cranberries
½ pint/300 ml water
6 oz/150 g sugar
1 oz/25 g butter

Put the cranberries and water in the crockpot and cook on
HIGH for 2 hours. Stir in the sugar and butter, cover and cook
on HIGH for 1 hour. If liked, the fruit and cooking liquid may
be sieved after cooking before the sugar and butter are added,
to give a smooth sauce.

Golden Fruit Sauce

1 lb/500 g canned pineapple chunks
1½ lb/750 g canned peach slices
1½ oz/40 g butter
4 oz/100 g redcurrant jelly
1 teaspoon/5 ml grated lemon rind
4 tablespoons/60 ml brandy

Drain the fruit and put the pineapple chunks and peach slices
into the crockpot. Add small pieces of butter, redcurrant jelly
and lemon rind. Cover and cook on LOW for 2–3 hours. Stir
in the brandy and serve warm over sponge puddings, milk puddings or ice cream.

Cheese Fondue

1 garlic clove
¼ pint/150 ml dry white wine
8 oz/225 g Gruyere cheese
8 oz/225 g Emmenthal cheese
1 oz/25 g cornflour
Pepper
Ground nutmeg

Cut the garlic clove in half and rub the inside of the crockpot with the cut sides. Put the wine into the crockpot and heat on LOW for 30 minutes. Grate both the cheeses and mix with the cornflour, pepper and nutmeg. Add to the wine and stir well. Cook on LOW for 1½ hours, stirring after the first 30 minutes. Serve from the crockpot, with each person dipping in spears of crusty bread. The fondue may be left to keep warm on LOW for 1–2 hours.

Chocolate Fondue

6 oz/150 g plain chocolate
12 oz/350 g sugar
½ pint/250 ml single cream
4 oz/100 g butter
Pinch of salt
2 tablespoons/30 ml Tia Maria liqueur

Break up the chocolate and put into the crockpot. Heat on LOW for 45 minutes until the chocolate has melted. Stir in the sugar, cream, butter and salt, and heat on HIGH for 10 minutes, stirring constantly. Stir in the liqueur and switch to LOW to keep the fondue warm. Use cubes of spongecake, marshmallows and fruit for dipping. Chunks of bananas or pineapple, or whole strawberies or maraschino cherries are particularly suitable.

Puddings

A number of puddings may be made very easily in a crockpot, and this can be useful if a main course is to be a simple grill or roast, or a cold meal, and a substantial pudding is needed which can be cooked during the day. The long slow cooking ensures a perfect blending of flavours for fruit dishes, and a soft creaminess in milk-based recipes. Many puddings can be successfully steamed without the necessity of constant watching and 'topping-up' with boiling water which is necessary when a pudding is steamed on a stove.

All kinds of milk puddings and custards may be cooked and the addition of evaporated milk will give a rich flavour. Custards should be steamed in moulds and this method will ensure a firm but softly-textured set. The crockpot is particularly valuable for preparing fruit compotes, as little liquid is necessary and flavours are concentrated. If you like cooked dried fruit, such as prunes or apple rings, for breakfast, try preparing them overnight in the crockpot.

If your pudding is to be cooked in a bowl or mould in boiling water in the crockpot, be sure that the container fits comfortably into the crockpot. A 1 pint/500 ml size is usually the right one to use, althought a larger but shallower container, such as a soufflé dish can sometimes be used.

Baked Apples

½ oz/15 g butter
4 cooking apples
4 oz/100 g soft brown sugar
4 oz/100 g seedless raisins
¼ pint/150 ml boiling water

Grease the base of the crockpot with the butter. Core the apples and run a sharp knife round the circumference to score the skin. Arrange the apples in the crockpot and fill the centres with a mixture of sugar and raisins. Pour in the boiling water. Cook on LOW for 4–5 hours.

Apples in Rum

4 apples
2 oz/50 g apricot jam
1 orange
3 fl. oz/75 ml water
4 oz/100 g sugar
3 tablespoons/45 ml rum

The best apples to use for this recipe are large crisp eating apples. Peel them, take out the cores and cut in half. Grease the crockpot with a little butter and put in the apples cut-side up. Over a low heat, simmer the apricot jam, grated rind and juice of the orange, water and sugar until the mixture is well blended and thick. Take off the heat and stir in the rum. Pour over the apples and cook on LOW for 4 hours. Serve hot or cold with cream.

Banana Rumba

1 oz/25 g butter
8 small bananas
2 oz/50 g soft brown sugar
1 oz/25 g desiccated coconut
3 fl. oz/75 ml rum
3 fl. oz/75 ml water

Use slightly under-ripe bananas for this recipe. Grease the crockpot with the butter. Peel the bananas and slice them in half lengthwise. Mix the sugar and coconut together. Arrange the bananas in layers in the crockpot, sprinkling of sugar mixture on top. Mix together the rum and water and pour over the fruit. Cook on LOW for 5 hours. Serve hot with cream.

Peaches in White Wine

8 peaches
½ pint/300 ml white wine
4 oz/100 g sugar
1 tablespoon/15 ml Kirsch

Peel the peaches and cut them in half, removing the stones. Put the sugar and wine into the crockpot, stir well, and heat on HIGH for 20 minutes. Put in the peaches, cut side down, and cook on LOW for 4 hours. Cool and stir in Kirsch just before serving. Serve with cream.

Pears in Red Wine

2 oz/50 g sugar
½ pint/300 ml red wine
6 medium pears
Rind of 1 lemon
1 oz/25 g flaked almonds

Eating pears which are just ripe are best for this dish. Put the sugar and wine into the crockpot, stir well, and heat on HIGH for 20 minutes. Meanwhile, peel the pears and leave them whole with the stalks on. Put into the crockpot, turning them in the wine to coat them well. Add the lemon rind in one piece. Cook on LOW for 5–6 hours, turning the pears twice during cooking to coat them in wine. Remove the lemon peel before serving, and scatter the almonds on the pears. Serve with cream.

Cider may be used instead of red wine.

Plums in Port

2 lb/1 kg small black plums
½ pint/300 ml port
1 slice of orange
4 cloves
4 oz/100 g sugar
1 cinnamon stick

Put the plums into the crockpot and cover with the port. Stick the cloves into the orange slice and add to the crockpot with the sugar and cinnamon stick. Cook on HIGH for 30 minutes and then stir well. Continue cooking on LOW for 2 hours. Remove the orange slice and chill the fruit before serving.

Poached Fruit

3 oz/75 g sugar
½ pint/300 ml water
1 lb/450 g fruit

The most suitable fruits for this method of cooking are plums, damsons, greengages, apricots, rhubarb and gooseberries. Prepare the fruit by wiping well, removing stems, etc., and put into the crockpot. Put the sugar and water in a saucepan and stir over heat until the sugar has dissolved and the syrup is boiling. Pour the syrup over the fruit and cook on LOW for 1–2 hours so that the fruit is tender but not broken.

Orange Prunes

1 lb/450 g large prunes
½ pint/300 ml orange juice
1 cinnamon stick
1 lemon

Put the prunes into the crockpot with the orange juice and cinnamon stick. The prunes should be just covered with liquid, and a little more orange juice or water may be added if necessary. Do not peel the lemon but cut it in thin slices. Arrange these over the prunes and cook on LOW for 6–8 hours. Remove the lemon slices before serving hot or cold. The prunes may be cooked overnight to serve at breakfast.

Dried Fruit Compôte

1 lb/450 g mixed dried fruit
1 slice of lemon
¼ pint/150 ml water

Use a mixture of prunes, pears, apricots and apples, or just one or two of these dried fruits. Put into the crockpot with the lemon slice and water. Cook on HIGH for 30 minutes and then on LOW for 5–6 hours. Remove the lemon slice before serving hot or cold. Some chopped nuts may be added to the fruit just before serving, or a spoonful or two of rum or brandy.

Summer Fruit Compôte

12 large plums
2 peaches
6 apricots
4 oz/100 g seedless grapes
¼ pint/150 ml water
4 oz/100 g sugar
1 oz/25 g honey
1 tablespoon/15 ml lemon juice
1 lemon

Cut the plums, peaches and apricots in half and remove the stones. Remove the grapes from their stems. Arrange the fruit in layers in the crockpot. Put the sugar and water in a saucepan and heat gently, stirring until the sugar has dissolved, and then bring to the boil. Remove from the heat and stir in the honey and lemon juice. Pour over the fruit in the crockpot. Do not peel the lemon but cut it in thin slices. Arrange the slices on top of the fruit. Cook on LOW for 5–6 hours. Remove the lemon slices and chill the fruit before serving with cream. This fruit mixture is also very good with yoghurt or commercial soured cream.

Apple Crumb Charlotte

6 apples
4 oz/100 g fresh white breadcrumbs
4 oz/100 g soft brown sugar
½ teaspoon/2.5 ml ground cinnamon
2 oz/50 g butter
½ pint/300 ml sweet applesauce

Use crisp eating apples for this recipe, which will retain their
shape when cooked. Peel the apples and slice them thinly.
Grease a crockpot with a little butter. Put in a layer of apples,
then breadcrumbs and sugar. Sprinkle with cinnamon and dot
with small pieces of butter. Repeat the layers and then pour on
the apple sauce. Cover and cook on LOW for 6 hours. Serve
with cream or brandy butter.

Fruit and Oat Crumble

1 lb/450 g cooking apples, rhubarb or gooseberries
4 oz/100 g soft brown sugar
2 oz/50 g plain flour
2 oz/50 g porridge oats
½ teaspoon/2·5 ml ground cinnamon
½ teaspoon/2·5 ml ground nutmeg
3 oz/75 g butter

Peel the apples, cut them in slices and put in the bottom of a greased crockpot. If using rhubarb, clean and cut into small pieces. Clean, top and tail gooseberries. Stir together the sugar, flour, oats and spices. Soften the butter slightly and work into the mixture until it is crumbly. Sprinkle over the fruit, cover and cook on LOW for 5–6 hours. Serve hot with cream, custard or ice cream.

Jam Sponge

2 oz/50 g jam
2 oz/50 g butter or margarine
2 oz/50 g caster sugar
1 egg
3 oz/75 g self-raising flour
A little milk

Grease a 1 pint/500 ml basin and put the jam in the base. Raspberry, strawberry or apricot jam may be used to give the pudding a distinctive flavour. Cream the fat and sugar until light and fluffy and gradually beat in the egg. Fold in the flour and add a little milk to make a smooth dropping consistency. Put the mixture on top of the jam in the basin, smooth the surface and cover with a foil lid. Put a jam-jar lid on the base of the crockpot and stand the basin on this. Pour boiling water into the crockpot to come half way up the sides of the basin and cook on HIGH for 3 hours. Turn out the pudding and serve with custard and some additional warm jam if liked.

Steamed Currant Pudding

4 oz/100 g self-raising flour
2 oz/50 g fresh white breadcrumbs
3 oz/75 g shredded suet
2 oz/50 g sugar
2 oz/50 g currants
¼ pint/150 ml milk

Stir together flour, breadcrumbs, suet, sugar and currants. Add the milk and mix well to make a soft dough. Grease a 1 pint/500 ml pudding basin and put in the mixture. Cover with a lid of foil. Put a jam-jar lid on the base of the crockpot and stand the basin on this. Pour boiling water into the crockpot to come half way up the sides of the basin. Cook on HIGH for 5 hours. Turn out and serve with butter and brown sugar.

Marmalade Pudding

8 slices white bread (large loaf)
2 oz/50 g butter
1½ oz/40 g marmalade
Pinch of ground nutmeg
1 pint/500 ml milk
1 oz/25 g sugar
2 large eggs

Remove the crusts from the bread slices. Spread each slice with butter and marmalade and sprinkle on a little nutmeg. Grease the crockpot with a little butter and arrange the bread in two layers. Warm the milk just to boiling point and stir in the sugar. Beat the eggs with a fork until broken up and pour on the warm milk. Strain this mixture over the bread. Put a piece of greaseproof paper on top of the crockpot under the lid. Cook on LOW for 3–4 hours. If you have a crockpot from which the stoneware lid can be lifted, remove the stoneware pot and sprinkle soft brown sugar thickly on top of the pudding. Brown under the grill to give a crisp topping.

Fruit Castles

4 oz/100 g butter
4 oz/100 g sugar
2 eggs
4 oz/100 g self-raising flour
Grated rind of 1 orange
3 oz/75 g sultanas
A little milk

Cream the butter and sugar until light and fluffy. Beat in the eggs one at a time with a little flour. Stir in the orange rind and sultanas, and a little milk with the rest of the flour to make a soft dropping consistency. Put into 8 greased castle pudding moulds and cover the tops with foil. Put into the crockpot and pour in enough boiling water to come half way up the moulds. Cook on HIGH for 2–3 hours. Turn out and serve with custard or a little warm apricot jam.

Lemon Sponge Pudding

3 eggs
1 teaspoon/5 ml grated lemon rind
3 tablespoons/45 ml lemon juice
1½ oz/40 g butter
½ pint/300 ml milk
6 oz/150 g sugar
1½ oz/40 g plain flour
Pinch of salt

Separate the eggs and beat the whites to stiff peaks. Beat the egg yolks and mix in the lemon rind and juice, softened butter and milk. Stir together the sugar, flour and salt, and add to the egg mixture, beating until smooth. Fold in the egg whites. Pour into the crockpot and cook on HIGH for 2–3 hours.

Ginger Syrup Pudding

2 oz/50 g plain flour
½ teaspoon/2·5 ml bicarbonate of soda
Pinch of salt
1 teaspoon/5 ml ground ginger
2 oz/50 g fresh white breadcrumbs
2 oz/50 g shredded suet
3 oz/75 g golden syrup
1 egg
A little milk

Grease a 1 pint/500 ml pudding basin. Sieve the flour, soda, salt and ginger, and stir in the breadcrumbs and suet. Stir in the syrup and lightly-beaten egg and mix well. Add a little milk if necessary to give a soft dropping consistency. Put into the basin and smooth the top. Cover with a lid of foil. Put a jam-jar lid on the base of the crockpot and stand the basin on this. Pour boiling water into the crockpot to come half way up the sides of the basin and cook on HIGH for 3–4 hours. Turn out the pudding and serve with some warm golden syrup or marmalade.

Chocolate Nut Pudding

2 oz/50 g butter or margarine
4½ oz/115 g sugar
1 egg
4 oz/100 g dry white breadcrumbs
1½ oz/40 g plain flour
1 teaspoon/5 ml baking powder
Pinch of salt
¼ pint/150 ml milk
2 oz/50 g plain chocolate
1½ oz/40 g chopped walnuts

Cream the butter and sugar. Add the egg and beat well. Work in the breadcrumbs, flour, baking powder, and salt. Put the milk and chocolate in a saucepan and heat gently until the chocolate has melted. Cool and add to the creamed mixture together with the nuts. Put into a greased 1 pint/500 ml soufflé dish. Put a jam-jar lid on the base of the crockpot and stand the basin on this. Pour boiling water into the crockpot to come half way up the sides of the dish and cook on HIGH for 3 hours. Serve with cream or ice cream.

Christmas Pudding

2 oz/50 g plain flour
½ teaspoon/2.5 ml baking powder
4 oz/100 g shredded suet
4 oz/100 g fresh white breadcrumbs
4 oz/100 g currants
1 oz/25 g mixed candied peel
4 oz/100 g raisins
4 oz/100 g soft brown sugar
½ teaspoon/2.5 ml ground mixed spice
1 egg
A little milk

Stir together the flour, baking powder, suet and breadcrumbs. Add the currants and chopped peel, raisins, sugar and spice. Mix with the egg and enough milk to give a soft dropping consistency. Put into a greased 1½ pint/1 litre pudding basin and cover with foil. Put a jam-jar lid on the base of the crockpot and stand the basin on this. Pour boiling water into the crockpot to come half way up the sides of the dish and cook on HIGH for 5-6 hours. Leave in the basin for 10 minutes before turning out. Serve with cream, custard or brandy butter. This is an economical pudding, but the fruit may be varied according to circumstances as long as the total weight is maintained. Sultanas and/or chopped block dates may be substituted for some of the other fruit, and a few chopped glacé cherries may be added.

Egg Custard

4 eggs
2 oz/50 g caster sugar
1 pint/500 ml milk
Pinch of ground nutmeg

Break the eggs into a bowl and mix with the sugar until the eggs are completely broken up. Heat the milk to just under boiling point. Pour on to the eggs and stir well. Strain into a greased 1½ pint/1 litre dish and sprinkle with the nutmeg. Cover with foil. Put a jam-jar lid on the base of the crockpot and stand the dish on this. Pour boiling water into the crockpot to come half way up the sides of the dish. Cook on LOW for 4 hours. For a special occasion, chill the egg custard in the dish. Sprinkle thickly with caster or soft brown sugar and put under the grill until the sugar caramelizes.

Cream Caramel

2 oz/50 g granulated sugar
4 tablespoons/60 ml water
4 eggs
2 oz/50 g caster sugar
1 pint/500 ml milk

Put the granulated sugar and water into a heavy pan and heat gently to dissolve the sugar. Boil until the mixture becomes brown caramel. Pour into a 1½ pint/1 litre soufflé dish or pudding basin, turning the dish so that the caramel is evenly distributed. Mix the eggs and caster sugar so that the eggs are well broken up. Heat the milk to just under boiling point and pour on to the eggs. Mix well and strain the mixture into the dish on top of the caramel. Cover with foil. Put a jam-jar lid in the bottom of the crockpot and stand the dish or basin on this. Pour in boiling water until it comes half way up the sides of the container. Cook on LOW for 5 hours. Leave to cool overnight and turn out carefully. Serve with cream.

Rice Pudding

3 oz/75 g pudding rice
2 oz/50 g sugar
1½ pints/750 ml milk
1 oz/25 g butter
Pinch of ground nutmeg

Grease the crockpot with a little of the butter. Put the rice into the crockpot wth the sugar and milk, and stir well. Cut the butter into thin flakes and put on to the mixture. Sprinkle with nutmeg. Cook on LOW for 6–8 hours. A creamier rice pudding can be made if some evaporated milk is substituted for part of the milk. Cooking time will be speeded up if the milk is brought to the boil before adding to the crockpot. To vary the rice pudding, cook a few sultanas or raisins in the mixture, or flavour with a little cocoa mixed to a paste with some of the milk before adding to the crockpot.

Jams and Pickles

The crockpot is very useful for preparing home-made sweet preserves and pickles. Many recipes require long, slow cooking to soften the fruit or vegetables and this can be a tiresome business as bottom heat may cause the contents of a preserving pan to catch and burn. This means constant attention and frequent stirring when preserves are made by the conventional methods. The preliminary cooking can take place overnight in the crockpot, or during the day when everyone is out of the house, and all-round heat will ensure the preserve will not burn. Vinegar-based pickles can be cooked completely in the crockpot, but jam needs a few minutes' boiling with sugar in an open saucepan to ensure a firm set. Marmalade is very good made in the crockpot, which ensures that the hard citrus peel is completely softened, giving a good set without the long hard boiling when sugar is added, which often results in syrupy marmalade with hard peel.

Try some of the suggested recipes first and then adapt your own favourites for crockpot use. Stone fruits, currants and gooseberries are suitable for crockpot cookery, but strawberries and raspberries will lose their attractive colour and fresh flavour during prolonged cooking.

Marmalade

2 lb/1 kg Seville oranges
1 lemon
3½ pints/2 l water
4 lb/2 kg sugar

Cut the oranges and lemon in halves and squeeze out the juice.
Take out the pips from the fruit and remove the pith from the
peel. Put the pips and pith into a small saucepan with ½ pint/
300 ml water and simmer for 1 hour. Meanwhile chop the peel
finely. Put into the crockpot with the fruit juices. Boil the
remaining water and pour over the peel. Cook on LOW for
8–10 hours. Put the peel and liquid into a large saucepan or
preserving pan. Add the sugar and the strained liquid from the
pips. Heat gently until the sugar dissolves, and then boil
rapidly to setting point. Test a spoonful of the marmalade on a
cold saucer. If it forms a skin and wrinkles when pushed with
a finger, the marmalade has reached setting point. Remove
from the heat and leave to stand for 15 minutes. Stir well, pour
into clean jars and cover.

Note
    Another method can be used for softening the peel, which is
good if you like to use the method of cooking large pieces of
fruit before chopping (lemon marmalade is often made this
way). Choose your favourite recipe and weigh the fruit. Wash
and dry the fruit and cut into halves or quarters. Put into the
crockpot and just cover with water. Cook on LOW for 10–12
hours or overnight. Drain off the water and use as part of the
liquid in the recipe.

Lemon Curd

4 oz/100 g butter
12 oz/350 g caster sugar
2 large lemons
2 eggs

Put the butter and sugar into a saucepan with the grated rind and juice of the lemons. Heat gently and stir until the sugar has dissolved. Leave until cold and beat in the eggs. Put into a bowl which will fit into the crockpot and cover with foil. Pour boiling water into the crockpot to come half way up the bowl. Cook on LOW for 4–5 hours. Stir well and put into jars, covering at once. Lemon curd will keep in a cool place for 2 months.

Summer Jam

2 lb/1 kg fruit
½ pint/300 ml water
2 lb/1 kg sugar

If you have little time for jam-making, the crockpot can be
used for the initial preparation of the fruit overnight. The jam
can then be finished off in about 10 minutes. Use plums, apricots, damsons, greengages, gooseberries or blackcurrants for
this recipe. Wash the fruit and remove stalks (or top and tail
gooseberries or blackcurrants). Put the fruit and water into the
crockpot and cook on LOW for 6–8 hours or overnight. Warm
the sugar and put into a large saucepan. Add the fruit and
liquid and stir over low heat so that the sugar dissolves. Bring
to the boil and boil rapidly for about 7 minutes. Put a spoonful
of the jam on to a cold saucer, leave to cool slightly and push it
gently with a finger. If the mixture forms a skin and wrinkles
when pushed, the jam is ready. Put into clean jars and cover at
once.

Apple Butter

5 lb/2·5 kg cooking apples
¾ pint/400 ml cider
1 lb/450 g soft brown sugar
1 lemon
1 orange
1 teaspoon/5 ml ground cinnamon
½ teaspoon/2·5 ml ground allspice
Pinch of ground cloves
Pinch of ground nutmeg

Use apples which cook easily to a purée such as Bramley's Seedling. Wipe the apples but do not peel them. Cut in quarters and take out the cores. Put into the crockpot with the cider and cook on HIGH for 1½ hours. Sieve the apples and liquid. Return the fruit purée to the crockpot with the sugar, grated rind and juice of the lemon and orange, and the spices. Cook on HIGH for 3–4 hours until thick and dark. Pour into warm jars and cover.

Apple Chutney

5 lb/2.5 kg apples
8 oz/225 g onions
1 pint/500 ml vinegar
½ oz/15 ml salt
8 oz/225 g stoned dates
8 oz/225 g sultanas
½ oz/15 ml ground ginger
1 lb/450 g Demerara sugar

Peel and core the apples, and peel the onions. Mince them coarsely. Put into the crockpot with the salt, finely chopped dates, sultanas, ginger and sugar. Stir well, cover and cook on LOW for 10 hours or overnight. Pour into warm jars and cover with vinegar-proof lids.

Gooseberry Chutney

3 lb/1.5 kg gooseberries
3 medium onions
8 oz/225 g sultanas
12 oz/350 g Demerara sugar
1½ pints/750 ml vinegar
½ oz/15 ml mustard powder
1 teaspoon/5 ml turmeric
1 teaspoon/5 ml ground ginger
Salt and pepper
Pinch of nutmeg

Top and tail the gooseberries and mince them coarsely with the onions. Add the sultanas, sugar, vinegar, mustard, turmeric and ginger. Put into the crockpot with a pinch each of salt, pepper and nutmeg. Stir well, cover and cook on LOW for 10 hours or overnight. Pour into warm jars and cover with vinegar-proof lids.

Plum Chutney

2½ lb/2·25 kg mixed plums
1 lb/450 g carrots
1 pint/500 ml vinegar
1 lb/450 g raisins
1 lb/450 g soft brown sugar
1 oz/25 g garlic
1 oz/25 g chillies
1 oz/25 g ground ginger
1½ oz/40 g salt

A mixture of all sorts of plums may be used for this chutney, and some damsons may be added too. Wipe them well and cut them in half. Take out the stones, and chop the plum flesh. Peel the carrots and mince them coarsely. Add them to the vinegar and put into the crockpot. Stir in the other ingredients, chopping the garlic and chillies finely. Cover and cook on LOW for 10 hours or overnight. Pour into warm jars and cover with vinegar-proof lids.

Rhubarb Chutney

2 lb/1 kg rhubarb
8 oz/225 g onions
1½ lb/700 g soft brown sugar
8 oz/225 g sultanas
1 teaspoon/5 ml mustard powder
1 teaspoon/5 ml pepper
1 teaspoon/5 ml ground mixed spice
1 teaspoon/5 ml ground ginger
1 teaspoon/5 ml salt
Pinch of cayenne pepper
1 pint/500 ml vinegar

Cut the rhubarb into 1 in./2.5 cm lengths. Chop the onions
very finely. Put all the ingredients into the crockpot and stir
well. Cook on LOW for 10 hours or overnight. Pour into warm
jars and cover with vinegar-proof lids.

Tomato Chutney

3 lb/1.5 kg green tomatoes
2 small cooking apples
2 medium onions
4 oz/100 g soft brown sugar
¾ pint/400 ml vinegar
2 teaspoons/10 ml salt
½ oz/15 g ground mixed spice

Put the tomatoes into boiling water and then skin them. Chop the tomatoes and put into the crockpot. Peel the apples and onions and chop them finely. Add the sugar, vinegar, salt and spice. Stir very well and cook on LOW for 10 hours or overnight. Pour into warm jars and cover with vinegar-proof lids.

Drinks

A crockpot is very useful for making hot drinks for small informal parties. The ingredients can be heated gently, blending the flavours of the spices into the main ingredients, and then the crockpot makes a container from which the drinks may be served and kept warm for second helpings. Mulled wine or a spiced punch can be assembled and left on LOW heat while you go for a walk, attend a match or visit a theatre, and it will be ready for drinking as soon as you get back.

Before making these drinks, check the size of your crockpot, as they vary considerably in capacity. Quantities can of course be halved for small crockpots or small parties. Serve hot drinks from pottery mugs, or from thick glass tankards containing a metal spoon to prevent cracking. A cinnamon stick can be put into each mug to use as a stirrer.

Mulled Wine

2 bottles red wine
½ pint/300 ml water
8 oz/225 g sugar
1 teaspoon/5 ml ground nutmeg
2 cinnamon sticks
1 orange
1 lemon

Put the wine, water, sugar and spices into the crockpot. Do not peel the fruit, but cut across in thin slices. Add to the crockpot, cover and heat on LOW for 2–3 hours. Serve from the crockpot and keep on LOW heat for second helpings.

Party Punch

2 bottles red wine
3 fl. oz/75 ml brandy
Peel of 1 orange
Peel of 1 lemon
3 oz/75 g soft brown sugar
2 teaspoons/10 ml ground mixed spice
2 small thin skinned oranges
12 cloves

Put the wine and brandy into the crockpot. Peel the orange and lemon thinly, and add to the wine with the sugar and spice. Stick the cloves into the whole oranges and add to the crockpot. Cover and heat on LOW for 2–3 hours. Serve from the crockpot and keep on LOW heat for second helpings.

Ski Punch (1)

6 oz/150 g sugar
¾ pint/400 ml water
½ cinnamon stick
½ teaspoon cardamom seed
6 cloves
1 oz/25 g sultanas
1 oz/25 g blanched almonds
1 lemon
1 bottle red wine
¼ pint/150 ml brandy or vodka

Put the sugar and water into a saucepan. Stir well and bring to
the boil so that the sugar dissolves. Put into the crockpot with
cinnamon stick, cracked cardamom seed, cloves, sultanas and
almonds. Do not peel the lemon but cut it in thin slices. Add to
the crockpot with the wine and brandy or vodka. Heat on LOW
for 2–3 hours. Serve from the crockpot and keep on LOW heat
for second helpings. Include a few sultanas and almonds in
each mug.

Ski Punch (2)

2 bottles port
¼ pint/150 ml brandy
12 cloves
2 teaspoons cardamom seeds
2 cinnamon sticks
4 oz seedless raisins

Put the port and brandy in the crockpot with the cloves, cracked cardamom seeds and cinnamon sticks, and add the raisins. Cover and heat on LOW for 2–3 hours. Serve from the crockpot and keep on LOW heat for second helpings.

Spiced Cider

1 bottle cider
½ pint/300 ml sweet white wine
2 oranges
1 cinnamon stick

Put the cider and wine into the crockpot. Slice the oranges with the peel on, and add to the wine with the cinnamon stick and cloves. Cover and heat on LOW for 2–3 hours. Serve from the crockpot and keep on LOW heat for second helpings.

Spiced Sherry

6 cloves
6 oz/150 g can frozen orange juice
½ pint/300 ml dry sherry
¾ pint/400 ml water
1 oz/25 g sugar
1 cinnamon stick
4 cloves
1 oz/25 g butter

Thaw the orange juice and mix with the sherry, water, sugar and spices. Cover and heat on LOW for 2–3 hours. Serve from the crockpot, topping each serving with a small piece of butter. Keep on LOW heat for second helpings.

Rum Punch

2 pints/1 l water
½ pint/300 ml dark rum
4 oz/100 g soft brown sugar
2 oz/50 g butter
1 cinnamon stick
2 cloves

Boil the water and put into the crockpot with the other ingredients. Stir well and heat on LOW for 3–4 hours. Serve in the crockpot and keep on LOW heat for second helpings.

Cider Punch

6 oz/150 g can frozen orange juice
¾ pint/400 ml water
1 bottle cider
5 cloves
2 cinnamon sticks
1 teaspoon/5 ml ground nutmeg
½ teaspoon/2.5 ml ground ginger
Orange slices

Thaw the orange juice and mix with the water, cider and spices.
Put into the crockpot, cover and heat on LOW for 3–4 hours.
Serve from the crockpot and keep on LOW heat for second
helpings. Garnish each serving with an orange slice.

Fruit Punch (non-alcoholic)

3 pints/1·5 l boiling water
6 tea bags
2 oz/50 g sugar
2 oz/50 g honey
½ pint/300 ml orange juice
½ pint/300 ml pineapple juice
1 orange

Pour the boiling water over the teabags in a jug. Cover and leave to stand for 5 minutes. Strain the liquid into the crockpot. Stir in the sugar, honey and fruit juices. Without peeling, cut the orange into thin slices. Add to the crockpot. Cover and heat on LOW for 3–4 hours. Serve from the crockpot and keep on LOW heat for second helpings.

Spiced Lemon Tea

4 pints/2 l boiling water
6 tea bags
4 oz/100 g sugar
12 cloves
½ teaspoon/2.5 ml whole allspice
1 cinnamon stick
2 lemons
1 orange

Boil half the water and pour over the teabags in a jug. Cover
and leave to stand for 10 minutes. Stain into the crockpot and
stir in the sugar and spices. Remove the peel very thinly from
the fruit and add to the crockpot. Squeeze out the fruit juice,
strain and add to the crockpot. Boil the remaining water and
add to the mixture. Cover and heat on LOW for 2–3 hours.
Serve from the crockpot and keep on LOW heat for second
helpings.

Mexican Coffee

1 oz/25 g cocoa
4 tablespoons/60 ml boiling water
4 oz/100 g sugar
2 pints/1 l hot strong coffee
6 cloves
2 cinnamon sticks
Peel of 1 orange
Peel of 1 lemon
¼ pint/150 ml double cream

Mix the cocoa to a paste with the boiling water. Add the sugar
and hot coffee and stir until well mixed. Put into the crockpot
with the spices. Cover and heat on LOW for 2–3 hours. Serve
from the crockpot, garnishing each serving with a piece of
orange peel and a piece of lemon peel and a spoonful of
whipped cream. Keep coffee warm on LOW heat for second
helpings.

Index